To kishorebhai,
with best wishes

— Rahul Shukla
January 18, 2012

MEASURE OF A MAN

By
Akash Shukla
with
Rahul Shukla

Llumina
Press

ISBN: 978-1-60594-291-9

Printed in the United States of America by Llumina Press

Library of Congress Control Number: 2008906907

To my Mom and Dad

1   How Would They Tell Me?

It was a cold, windy afternoon in March 2002 when I called my friend John Nastus and asked him to meet me at the mall. John and I were going to see the new Jodie Foster movie, *Panic Room*.

Bridgewater Commons is a vibrant shopping haven and a popular hangout for teenagers. It has hundreds of stores and a movie theater complex. The mall is always bursting with a young crowd. The girls dress up in bold, provocative ways, with their low cut blouses, their belly buttons showing, and their pants hanging low, Britney Spears-style. To a sixteen-year-old boy, the pretty girls were a feast to the eyes.

My learner's permit required that I have an adult driver in the front seat, so my dad had to accompany me for the ride. Once we reached there, Dad took the car back home. "Come back in three hours," I told him.

I looked for John at the terrace entrance door. There was no sign of him. As I waited for John at the ticket window, I saw two pretty girls standing in line to buy movie tickets. They looked about sixteen or seventeen. The blonde was wearing a white blouse and a rather short black skirt; the brunette wore a blue sporty tank-top with white athletic pants. The brunette was five feet one, thin and petite. As I was admiring how pretty she was, she suddenly turned her head and looked at me. I smiled at her. Her face tightened into a stern look. She quickly turned her face away. She then turned to her friend and whispered something in her ear. Her friend gave me a quick look and turned her face away. Maybe they were wondering, "Why is this 'kid' checking us out?"

Yes, I was sixteen, but I was only four feet eleven inches tall. I never looked my age. Girls always got uncomfortable if they saw me checking them out. Most of them did not even notice me, and those who did would get uncomfortable that some "young kid" was checking them out. Being short was okay most of the time but very painful other times. I knew there were some things in life that we select for ourselves and can change at will- things such as our profession and our friends. Some other things are selected for us by destiny- things such as whether you are black or white or whether you have normal height or are very short. I was still hoping that I had not finished growing. Many well-meaning friends and relatives would tell me, "Mr. So and So's son grew four inches between the ages of sixteen and eighteen." I hoped the same would happen to me, but somehow did not think it was likely.

When I was five, I was the same height as my friends. By the time I was eight years old, I was a little shorter than kids of my age. As per my pediatrician's recommendation, my parents took me to see an endocrinologist. He expressed concern and asked us to see him a year later.

By the time I was ten, I was noticeably shorter than other kids. My parents took me to another specialist. After doing several blood tests and a hand x-ray, the doctor told my parents that my hormone level was normal. He predicted my final height to be five feet three inches. As I found out later from my parents, the doctor recommended against hormone treatment. There was no solid scientific evidence at that time that children without hormone deficiencies would benefit from daily hormone shots, but there was a possibility of unforeseen side effects.

When I was twelve, we went to see yet another specialist, Dr. Garibaldi in Beth Israel Hospital. He performed a four-hour test to see whether my blood would react favorably with the introduction of growth hormones. The diagnosis was the same from Dr. Garibaldi. He said, "In your case, I'm not sure if the growth hormones would help, but I'm afraid they might hurt. Be happy with your predicted height of five feet three, and then get platform shoes." We came home and thought that the matter was concluded.

But it was not.

In the next few years, I grew even more slowly. Until high school, my height was not an issue. In middle school, I would go to the "teen night" dances, where girls used to dedicate songs to me. When I went to high school, I had a difficult time finding a girl to go to the Winter Ball with me. My classmates were always making jokes about my height. I would laugh it away by telling them that 'Good things come in small packages'. I knew that if I joked about my height, it would make it less tempting for them to do the same. When I ran for sophomore class vice president, I read my campaign speech while standing on a telephone book and that made everybody laugh. The laughter did not turn into a lot of votes, though.

By the time I was fifteen, reaching five feet three inches did not look promising. We came across another expert, Dr. Oberfield, at Columbia Presbyterian Hospital. I knew this meant one more trip to the hospital, several more blood tests, and a bone age x-ray. A bone age is done to determine the chronological age of a person. It is done by taking an x-ray of the left wrist and hand in order to compare a person's bone maturity to that of other children of the same sex and age. It helps determine a child's growth potential.

Based on the test results, Dr. Oberfield would tell me whether or not it was too late to start with the hormone therapy treatment. I had noticed that my voice was changing and my mustache was beginning to thicken. Somehow, I knew it was not likely that Dr. Oberfield would have good news for us.

I was keeping myself busy singing in the choir and writing for the school newspaper. Singing brought inner joy to me. Whether I was in choir class, or walking from my bedroom to the family room, I'd always be singing. My height was not something that I thought about all the time. In fact, only when I was the recipient of rude comments would I think about my height. That, and when girls my age treated me as if I was a little kid. What had happened at the Bridgewater Commons on a wintry afternoon in 2002 was not so uncommon for me anymore. The pretty girls always turned their faces away. If they looked back, it was with a look of curiosity and slight contempt. I was tired of being short. The growth spurt I was waiting for better happen soon, I kept saying to myself.

Then came the call from Dr. Oberfield. I would find out about it a few days later. It was six thirty in the evening when Mom answered the phone. She kept shaking her head in disbelief. She said, "Can you hold for a second? I need to get my husband on the line." She went to Dad in the family room. "It's Dr. Oberfield," she said. "It's not good news." Dad picked up another phone. Dr. Oberfield explained to both of them that based on my hand x-ray, it appeared that my growth plates were fused.

"What does that mean?" asked Dad.

"Well, he has finished growing," she replied.

"Are you sure there is no more growth to come?" asked Dad.

She said, "Let us say that he has achieved 98 percent of his final height."

"What about hormone treatment?" Mom asked.

"I'm afraid it's too late for that. And even if we had done it earlier, I don't know what results we would have gotten," Dr. Oberfield replied.

Once they hung up the phone, they sat quietly on the sofa. They did not say a word for a long time. Then Mom started sobbing. "How will we tell this to Akash?" she said.

2   We Learn About the Surgical Procedure

D r. Oberfield's call changed everything. Until that call, Mom and Dad had hoped that somehow things would work out. But the doctor said, "Akash has reached 98 percent of his final height."

Mom said to Dad, "That means there is some more growth to come."

"Yeah, 2 percent of four-eleven," Dad said. My parents thought there was one more inch to come. They did not realize that Dr. Oberfield was letting them down easy. She didn't want to say it was over. In any case, they knew that under the best of circumstances there was only an inch more; under the worst-case scenario, my current height was it. I was four feet eleven inches. We had known I was going to be short, but not this short.

I later found out that Mom and Dad spent the next few days in great agony. They hadn't broken the news to me yet. One night in March 2002, they both came to my room. I was standing near my armoire, changing into my night suit.

"We need to talk to you Son," Dad said.

"Yeah, Dad. What is it?" I was in my usual happy-go-lucky mood. I had no idea what my parents were about to tell me.

Dad took a deep breath and said, "We heard from Dr. Oberfield. She looked at your latest x-rays and it's bad news. She thinks you have reached your final height."

I stared at Mom and Dad, not sure if I had heard them right. "What?" I said incredulously.

"Yeah, Beta," said Mom, using the Indian word for "son." Her eyes welled with tears. She knew what a heartbreak this would be for a young man. "This is your final height- but so what? It's not the end of the world."

"But it can't . . . " I said in disbelief. "No, Dad." I looked at him and said in a pleading voice, "It can't be," as if Dad could somehow fix this for me. He had a sad stare in his eyes. I knew this time there was nothing he or Mom would be able to do to fix this.

"I am sorry, Son," Dad said.

By now, the information they just gave me was settling in. I shook my head and said, "This can't be happening." Mom held my hand. I said to her, "Why would God do this to me? What have I done?"

"It is not your fault," Mom said in a cracking voice.

I covered my face with my hand as a slow sob came out. I put my head on Mom's shoulder. I looked at Dad and asked again, "Why? Dad, why?" Dad kept nodding his head, as if to tell me that he understood- but there was nothing he could do. We hugged one another and cried for half an hour.

In my younger years, doctors had told us that I might not get much taller than five feet two inches. We had grudgingly accepted that five feet two was not all that bad. At four feet eleven, it would be tough going through life.

Our sobs filled the room. Mom and Dad kept telling me that my personality would carry me through. But I'm sure neither Mom nor Dad fully believed what they were saying.

The next few months were filled with sadness and restlessness. In this day and age of modern technology, where it seems that every complex problem has a solution, why couldn't my situation be resolved? How come there wasn't an answer?

I did not know this at the time, but at work, Dad was doing continuous research on the web: "increase height," "lengthen height," "become taller." He kept using various phrases on Yahoo's search engine. He kept reading article after article on the internet. Day after day, he found nothing useful. He remembered seeing something on TV about surgically increasing height. He tried many phrases with the word *surgery* and *height* but got nowhere. He later realized that he was not using the right phrase. He needed to use *"limb lengthening."* Then one evening, before leaving his office, he sat down to do some more research on the internet and this time used the phrase, *"short stature."* Bingo. That took him to *limb lengthening*, which led him to an article about how a doctor at Mount Sinai Hospital in Baltimore did a surgery to increase height. Dad quickly sent an e-mail through the hospital's website and asked for the contact information of the doctor. That was on May 2, 2002.

For the next three days, he was in overdrive. There was a glimmer of hope. In two more days, he knew the name of the doctor at Mount Sinai who did this surgery: Dr. Dror Paley. It became clear from Dad's research that this was the top orthopedic surgeon in the world for this specialized surgery. Dad composed a very personal letter. He knew that many doctors were not comfortable doing surgery like this. Many think that one should be happy with what God has given to you. If God gives you pneumonia, doctors don't mind prescribing antibiotics to get rid of it. But with height, many think you should simply leave it alone. Dad did not know where Dr. Paley stood philosophically, so he poured his heart out. Here is the letter he sent to Dr. Paley:

From Rahul Shukla

To: dpaley@Lifebridgehealth.org

5/6/2002 08:55 a.m.

Subject: Can you help my son with short stature

Dear Dr. Paley,

I am writing this letter to seek advice for my son, Akash. Akash is fifteen years and eight months old. He is four feet eleven inches tall and, according to a bone x-ray, has reached his final height. I recently read an article on the internet on "Lengthening for Stature in Normally Proportioned People." Up until that article, I had thought that this procedure was done only on people with disproportion. When I called the number on the article at the University of Maryland, they told me to call you. This morning, I talked to your office and they suggested that I send you an e-mail.

 Here is some additional information:

Doctors recognized Akash's slow growth early on. Ever since he was eight, we saw many specialists. There was no hormone deficiency. His height at that time was predicted to be five feet two inches and with luck, five feet four inches. We had opted not to treat him with hormones because there was not much evidence that people without deficiencies would be helped with the treatment. In the last twelve months, he has developed full pubic hair, his voice has changed, and he has a light mustache. Dr. Oberfield in New York did one more blood test and bone x-ray in March and told us that Akash, at four feet eleven inches, has reached his final height. When we told this to Akash, he sobbed uncontrollably. He is heartbroken over this and so are we. My wife Meena and I have only one son. Life has been very kind to us for all these many years, and we foolishly thought that with hard work and tenacity, we could always get the best for our son. God has humbled us profoundly.

Akash is otherwise in good general health. He is in the tenth grade. He is a gentle, sensitive kid with a great sense of humor. He was very popular in school until three years ago. His short height has made him extremely self-conscious. He now has very few friends at school.

My own height is five feet five inches. Meena is four feet eleven inches. On my mother's side, there have been quite a few short men (five feet to five feet two). I am originally from India. I have an MS in Industrial Engineering. We live in Warren, NJ. I own two manufacturing companies in Piscataway, NJ. 'S.S. White Technologies' makes flexible shaft products for auto and aircraft. 'S.S. White Medical' makes surgical tools, devices, etc. for orthopedic surgery.

We do not know if Akash would be a good candidate for limb extension. The article on the web said that this would be considered a cosmetic surgery, would take five to six months in a wheelchair, would mean a lot of pain for the patient, and a cost upwards of $70,000. I think we can handle all of these- although the pain part is something that Akash has to decide for himself. If this is feasible, our goal would be to gain two to two-and-a-half inches. The rest he can do with platform shoes and be close to five feet three.

Doctor, in this world full of many sad tragedies, what is happening with my son is not the end of the world. We still, like any parents, want to do everything humanly possible to seek happiness for our son. Limb lengthening is the last option we need to explore. After that, we will accept God's will with as much grace as we are capable of.

Please let me know if we need to make an appointment and come visit you.

Thank you,
Sincerely,
Rahul Shukla
President/CEO
S.S. White Technologies
www.sswt.com

Dad sent this e-mail at 8:55 on the morning of May 6, 2002. He didn't expect an answer for at least a few days. But the response came in at 10:34 that evening. Dad read it the next morning when he went to work. His heart leapt with joy. At the very least, he had connected with an expert.

Dr. Paley said in his e-mail, "We do not do this surgery until Akash is finished growing. I would suggest you come in to let me evaluate him and obtain x-rays."

He had signed the e-mail

Dror Paley, MD FRCS; Director, Rubin Institute for Advance Orthopedics; Co-Director, International Center for Limb Lengthening; Professor of Orthopedics: University of Maryland.

Looking at all the titles, Dad looked towards the sky and sent a silent thank-you to God. Dad knew he had located a superbly qualified doctor. For the first time in months, Dad felt a little inner peace. The helplessness our family had felt in our hearts for the last few months was destroying us from inside out. Now there was an option.

Dad started reading a lot on the procedure. It became clear that this wasn't an easy procedure. They insert a telescoping rod called an ISKD (Intra Skeletal Kinetic Distractor) inside your tibia bone, the main bone between your knee and your ankle. Once they insert this telescoping rod down the center of the tibia, they cut the tibia into two pieces. The secondary shinbone, the fibula, also has to be cut into two. The telescoping rod is then fastened securely onto the bone. A controlled daily ankle motion would cause the telescopic rod to extend. The ratcheting mechanism would prevent it from moving backwards. The rod would extend every day by one millimeter (about one-twenty-fifth of an inch). The body is fooled into believing that there is a normal injury and the fracture needs to be mended. The body starts growing new bone to fill the crack, except we keep moving the rod every day. Thus, instead of filling the crack, the body is fooled into continually making new bone. The muscles, arteries, and nerves have to stretch and grow by themselves. Only the bone would be cut; everything else is capable of stretching up to a point.

The first time Dad read the description of the surgery online, he covered his eyes with his hands and wept quietly in his office. "My God," he said. "In order to grow a few inches, you have to cut your leg bones in half." But at least there was an alternative.

Dad had told Mom about his e-mail to Dr. Paley, but had not described the procedure. Then one evening, he said to Mom, "Let me tell you about the procedure." When he explained the procedure, her jaw dropped.

"That sounds horrible," she said. "I don't think it would be worth it."

Dad said, "Why reject it now? Let us take a scientific approach. We gather all the facts and then evaluate the risk. We can decide to say 'no' any time between now and the surgery. If we say 'no' now, we will stop gathering the information."

Mom knew how much emotional pain I was in. She said, "All right. Let's continue looking into this."

Next, they had to find out if I was interested in this or not. When Dad came to talk to me, I was walking into my bathroom, getting ready to take a shower. Dad walked into the bathroom. He said, "You know, I can find a way where you can add two to three inches to your height."

My eyes lit up. "Really?" I said.

"Yes, but it is not an easy procedure," Dad said.

"I don't care. Tell me what it is."

"After I tell you how it is done, you probably will not want to do it." Dad was building up the suspense, but also preparing me for the shock of the process. If he hadn't, I might've rejected it as soon as I heard about it. Dad wanted me to give it a fair consideration.

"So here it is, Diku," Dad said. Diku is a loving abbreviation for the word "son" in Gujarati, my father's mother tongue.

Dad said, "They put a rod inside your bone, and then cut the bone in half. The rod moves the bone apart. Your body starts mending the fracture, but you move the bones apart every day and fool your body into making new bone. You can get two to three inches of height. Once the procedure is over, you will not even know that it was done."

I needed to sit down. I closed the toilet seat and collapsed on it.

Dad held my hand. He had tears in his eyes. He said, "It sounds pretty horrible, but it can fix something we thought was unfixable."

I looked at him. I was all shaken up. "Do you think it would hurt a lot?"

"I think it would- more than anything you can ever imagine. But then the pain would go away, and the increase in height would stay with you forever." Dad was holding back tears. He said, "You don't have to decide now. I just want you to know that there is an option."

I closed my eyes for a few seconds, took a deep breath, and then whispered, "I think this is very good news."

3 The Doctor Who Can Make Me Taller

I was pretty confused the next few nights. Yes, there was an answer, but it just sounded horrific. I wanted to know a lot more about the procedure. Dad would say, "Just think about whether this is even worth considering. We will find out the details later." I only later found out that he did not want us to look at the pictures of the procedure too soon. He thought the family should talk about it for a few days, get over the shock of the concept, and then look at the website.

The concept was pretty intense. To fracture your bone into two and then pull it apart every day- this sounded nothing short of the worst kind of a torture.

Dad was reading up on all of this a lot. One day, he sat Mom and me at the kitchen computer and signed on to the website of a company called "Orthofix" at www.orthofix.com. "Let us look at how this thing works- but," he said, "just because we check this out does not mean it is worth doing. We are just gathering knowledge."

It was one of the strangest experiences of my life. On one hand, I was happy that there seemed an answer to my impossible problem. On the other, I was frightened to death thinking about screwing those metal parts into my bones.

"What if something goes wrong?" Mom asked.

Dad had no answer. He said, "Let us write down all our questions. We will find answers to them, one by one."

How much would this cost, we were wondering. Dad said he thought the initial estimate was $70,000. But we knew that the cost was not yet a factor in our decision-making process. If it was not a safe procedure, even if it was done for free, it was meaningless. On the other hand, if it could make me a couple of inches taller, it would be nothing short of a miracle, and Mom and Dad would gladly spend that or a much bigger amount. It was a two-part decision-making process. In part one, Mom, Dad, and I would collectively decide if we thought the procedure was safe. The second part of the decision process was all on my shoulders. Did I want to undergo the most horrific pain any human being can ever undergo?

In June 2002, many of my relatives from England and Canada came to New Jersey for Mom and Dad's surprise twenty-fifth wedding anniversary. I talked to some of my relatives and asked for their opinion. Most of them were shocked that I would even consider such a surgery. "Be happy with what you have," many said. I was getting confused. Then Dad got a call from India. His mom was in the hospital, and her heart was failing. Dad rushed to India. He called us three days later. Grandma was in a coma and not likely to survive. Mom and I took the next plane to India.

It seemed that Grandma was not going to make it. I was very close to her. Suddenly, my height was not on my mind. Grandma was in a coma for a few days. She needed a new heart valve. The surgeon said, "There is only a 30 percent chance that she will come out of the surgery alive."

"Why do the surgery, then?" we asked.

The surgeon said, "If you do not do it, there is 100 percent chance that she will not survive." Grandma was eighty-four. No one in the hospital thought her body would be able to withstand the shock of open-heart surgery.

Miracles do happen. The surgery went well. Then Grandma came out of the coma. A few days later, we put her in a wheelchair and we pushed her chair to the prayer area in the hospital. Our entire extended family- some forty people- stood there in front of the statue of Lord Krishna. Everyone was thanking God with gratitude in our hearts and tears in our eyes. We came back to the USA in mid-August. Somehow, there was new optimism in me. I was ready to go see Dr. Paley at Sinai Hospital in Baltimore and find out more about this gruesome surgery.

Dror Paley, MD, is director of the Rubin Institute for Advanced Orthopedics at Sinai Hospital and co-director of the ICLL. His is also a professor of orthopedic surgery at the University of Maryland. Dr. Paley was the first North American orthopedic surgeon to study with Professor Ilizarov in the USSR. He introduced the Ilizarov method to the United States and Canada in 1985. He also trained in Italy with Professor DeBastiani, the founder of the Orthofix Method, as well as with Drs. Cattaneo and Catagni, the first surgeons to use the Ilizarov methods in Europe. Dr. Paley graduated from the University of Toronto Medical School and trained in surgery at the Johns Hopkins Hospital and in orthopedic surgery at the University of Toronto Hospitals. Dr. Paley completed subspecialty training in hand surgery, trauma surgery, and pediatric orthopedic surgery after his residency. He is also one of the first orthopedic surgeons to take six months of subspecialty training in limb lengthening and reconstruction in Italy and the USSR.

E-mail: dpaley@lifebridgehealth.org

Dr. Paley was a very busy man. When mom called for an appointment in late August, the first available slot was on October 25. By the time the appointment date was approaching, Baltimore was in the news a lot. In the first three weeks of October 2002, several sniper attacks took place in the Baltimore/Washington region. Ten people were killed and three critically wounded. Someone was randomly shooting people in and around the Baltimore/Washington metropolitan area and along Interstate 95 in Virginia.

Two days before my appointment, we sat down to discuss whether we should keep the date or not. In a way, it was time for us to start displaying courage. If a fear like this would slow us down, how would we deal with the gruesome surgery?

As we were driving from New Jersey to Baltimore on October 25, we heard on the radio that John Allen Muhammad and Lee Boyd Malvo had been arrested the previous day. We were still cautious. At the Sinai hospital, the three of us ran from the car to the main building.

We reached the hospital at ten a.m. The appointment was for ten thirty a.m. We took the elevator to the second floor. As soon as the elevator door opened, I saw a patient with an external fixator. (I did not know at that time what it was called.) It was made of circular plates. It surrounded his leg. The lower ring was one inch above the ankle, the upper one an inch below the knee, and they were bolted into the leg with large bolts sticking out. I quickly looked away. For a moment I thought I was going to faint. "Did you see that Dad?" I asked.

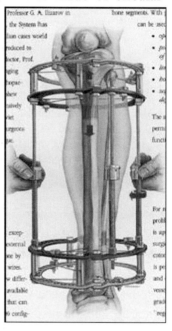

"Of course not," said Dad. He is the real chicken in our family. The very sight of blood gets him dizzy. My Grandma enjoys telling this story when years ago, she had a pimple-like infection with a pus pocket on her back. Dad took his mom to the doctor. The doctor asked Dad to hold Grandma's shoulder while he took a surgical knife and cut open the small pocket to let out the pus. The pulsating pain was gone. Grandma felt better right away. The doctor put medicated pads on the cut and put a band-aid-like tape. The whole procedure took less than two minutes. Dad reluctantly had to get a glimpse of what the doctor was doing. As Dad and Grandma got out of the doctor's office, Dad started looking pale. His legs looked wobbly, and then he fell hard on the road. His mom had to help him get up, hire a rickshaw, and get Dad home. She says laughingly, "If you are not well, don't ask for Rahul's help; you will end up looking after him."

Mom and I were mindful of Dad's weakness. There were a number of patients with these rings screwed in around their legs. Dad was working very hard not to catch even a glimpse. Mom was concerned. "Rahul, make sure you do not look at that," she said.

I said, "Dad, thank God for ISKD. I would never, in a million years, go with the external fixator."

We had all taken a lot of reading material with us. We started reading. Two hours later, a beautiful nurse called my name and took me to get a whole body x-ray. The x-ray would be done at actual scale for my entire lower body.

After one more hour of waiting, a young doctor asked me to follow him into the examination room. He was Dr. Paley's associate. He looked at the lower body x-ray and said, "To maintain good body proportion, it would be better to lengthen the tibia instead of the femur."

"Are Tibia and Femur like Starsky and Hutch?" I asked.

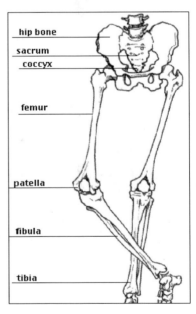

He did not laugh. "Tibia," he said, "is the bone between the ankle and the knee, and the femur is the bone between the knee and the thigh."

The young doctor then left and said Dr. Paley would be with us in a moment. It was already three p.m. Every now and then, we saw Dr. Paley walk by the room. We could recognize him from the pictures we had seen of him on the internet. An hour later, he finally came in the examination room. He was a tall, fairly fit man. He looked a little like Bruce Willis, which did not inspire our confidence in him. He talked in short sentences in an assertive tone. You could feel right away that you were in the presence of a world authority. "Am I a good candidate for limb lengthening?" was the question on my mind.

"Yes, you are" he said. "The ISKD can increase your height by up to three inches." He said, "Until ISKD, the doctors used external fixators but there is a high chance of getting the pins (screws) infected. The external fixator would give you the same results but with much more pain." Then he said, "I do not use the external fixator for this surgery."

I asked him how long I would be in a wheelchair. He said, "You will be allowed only restricted movement for the first three months, while the lengthening is occurring. Then, for six weeks after that, you will be completely bedridden."

I did not like the second part of that sentence at all. I said, "I'd sooner die of boredom than go through this surgery."

Mom looked at me somewhat impatiently. "Akash, you are worried about boredom but let us first ask about how safe this procedure is."

Dr. Paley said the procedure was very safe. He said any surgery has risks attached to it, but there were no unusual risks. Then Dad started asking questions. "How many such surgeries have you done?"

Dr. Paley said "Hundreds." Then he said, "Let me put it this way- of all the surgeries done in this country, 90 percent are done by me."

"Have any of your patients lost a limb as a result of this surgery?" Dad asked.

"No."

"Has anyone left the hospital with less range of motion then when they came in?" Dad asked.

"No," said Doctor Paley. But then he added, "Listen, have there been complications? Yes. But have we been able to take corrective action for them? The answer is also yes."

"What kind of complications?" Mom wanted to know.

"The first one is infection. If the rod gets infected, we would have no choice but to take the rod out. That would mean you spent the money for the surgery but did not get the increase in height. Second," he said, "is non-union." His tone changed a bit. "Once you create a gap at the point of the fracture, it is your body's turn to start creating new bone and mending the break. If the fractured bones do not mend, that is called non-union.

"What do we do then?" Mom asked.

"Well, we go in and fix it. We can do bone grafting. Once again, the loss is only financial as these procedures would cost additional money."

I asked, "I am a runner. Would I be able to run after the surgery?"

"I can't see why not," he said.

"How much taller would I get?" I asked.

He said, "Two inches is a no-brainer, but you could get up to three inches. Of course, you can do one surgery on the tibia and later a second one on the femur to get a total of six inches, but," he said, "no one has ever come back for the second surgery." We would only find out in the next two years why this was the case.

Dr. Paley wanted to wrap up the meeting. "This is completely doable. You will be three inches taller," he said confidently. He then said, "My secretary can put you in touch with a guy just like you. He lives in Canada. He took a year off before college. He was five feet tall. Now he is five feet, three inches." Dr. Paley got up to indicate that the meeting was coming to an end. "Come back in six months to discuss this more." He shook our hands and walked out. I looked at Mom and Dad. There was serene joy on their faces. I looked at my watch. It was six p.m. We were not angry about the long wait.

As we were driving home from Maryland, the joy I felt in my heart was difficult to describe. I knew that in the next few years I could be three inches taller. I would change what I thought could never be changed. Even if I decided not to go through with the surgery, at least it would be *my* decision. I realized that my sadness of the last few years wasn't all about my short height, but about the helplessness to do anything about it.

As we were driving on the New Jersey Turnpike towards home, I did not feel helpless anymore. Something that I thought was controlled by destiny was now under my control.

4   Was It Too Late for Hormone Treatment?

The next few months went by fast. We were still not all that sure whether this was the right thing to do, but Mom, Dad, and I were on a knowledge search mission. We were reading everything we could find on this subject.

Mom and Dad were still hoping that a miracle was going to happen and that I would shoot up several inches in a matter of months.

In March 2003, Dad went to New Orleans to attend the AAOS show (American Association of Orthopedic Surgery). In 1999, Dad's company had acquired a small manufacturing company that made orthopedic surgical tools. With the company came a few very knowledgeable technical people who understood the orthopedic field inside out. By 2003, Dad had started talking the language used by orthopedic surgeons. At the New Orleans Show, Dad went with their VP of Sales, Brian Parlato, and their orthopedic product manager, Glenn Rupp. The first two days, Dad spent working on his company's products. The last day, he asked Glenn to walk with him and went to the booth of Orthofix- the company that manufactured the limb-lengthening device called ISKD. Dad found their product development engineer, introduced himself as the president of S.S. White, and told the man, "I am talking to you as a father. My son is considering going through limb lengthening surgery. Can you educate me as to how this works?"

For the next half an hour, Dad got a very personal and very detailed lesson on the hardware, as well as the medical procedure, for using the ISKD. Glenn Rupp asked a lot of questions himself. Glenn is quite an expert on IM rods. Intramedullary (IM) rods are used to align and stabilize fractures. IM rods are inserted into the bone marrow canal in the center of the long bones of the extremities, such as the femur and the tibia. Glenn told Dad that ISKD was nothing more than a more sophisticated IM rod. Dad's company made a complete kit to remove the IM rods made by various manufacturers. Glenn's knowledge on IM rods was impeccable. He said to Dad, "In my opinion, this is a completely safe procedure. It would be as if your son had fractured his two legs in a ski accident- not that you would want such a thing, but if that happened, you would not think that it was a debilitating injury. You would know that it would get fixed."

Dad came home and shared all of that with Mom and me. There were times when Mom's resolve would get weak. "Why does height matter so much?" she would ask. "Look at me- I am only four feet eleven inches."

Dad would tell her, "There are different standards for women. Women are not judged harshly for being short. For men, it sucks."

They had both decided that once they verified it was a safe surgery, they would let it be my decision. Neither one of them wanted to go ahead with this but still were happy that we had the option.

It was May 6, 2003. I was sleeping in my bedroom and I heard a scream from Mom. It was six in the morning. I ran to Mom and Dad's bedroom. Dad was barely standing up in his bathroom, struggling to keep on his feet, then buckling and falling down. Mom was holding on to him. "Hold Dad," she said and ran to call 911.

No one knew Dad was a candidate for heart attack!

The ambulance took him to the hospital. At first they were not sure, but then the blood test that night confirmed the heart attack. The next morning, they moved him to another hospital and did the angiography. His right coronary artery was 100 percent blocked. Thankfully, he did not need a surgery. A metal stent was inserted in his right coronary artery. Dad came home in three days. Nothing was the same anymore.

A month later, Dad was almost back to normal. Then he noticed a lump on his thyroid. Initial tests were non-conclusive. Our family doctor, Dr. Goyal, suspected thyroid cancer. The first biopsy was inconclusive. Mom had gone into her problem-solver mode. She wanted to find a top doctor in the tri-state area to look at Dad's thyroid. It was a different doctor every week. The biopsy was still coming out inconclusive, but a renowned cancer surgeon at New York Presbyterian said he thought it was *not* cancer and that it would go away by itself. Just then, Dad was due for a follow-up stress test to make sure the stent had not clogged.

Dad found a new doctor. When he came back from the test, he said, "The doctor did not seem to follow the right procedure." Then the new doctor called and said, "The arteries seemed clogged again. Let us schedule another angiography." All this happened in less than three months. Mom called another cardiologist, this time our close friend Dr. Singal. He sent Dad to a fourth cardiologist in Lenox Hill Hospital. By October, we found out that the thyroid tumor had gone away by itself and Dad did not have any more clogged arteries.

We were greatly relieved. During these months, I had not given any thought to whether the leg surgery was the right thing. Dad was feeling okay now and I was back to worrying about whether to let doctors cut my legs or not.

I was in eleventh grade. I had started to apply for colleges. I needed to write a college essay. I thought about writing about my being selected as madrigal singer. It was a big deal for me. After being rejected for two years in a row, it had finally happened. But I also knew that my being selected for madrigal singer would not really make interesting reading. My agonizing choice as to whether to go ahead with the limb lengthening surgery was another story. It would be a novel subject- and it would allow me to pour my heart out.

Dad handed me a good quotation, called the "Serenity Prayer." It said:

"God, grant us the serenity to accept the things we cannot change, courage to change the things we can, and wisdom to know the difference."

It was a fitting prayer and yet with a twist. Should I show courage in changing my height or show wisdom in knowing that it couldn't be changed? While I was still struggling with that question, I wrote a good essay for my college application. It was heartfelt and sincere.

I had applied to nine colleges. I wanted to study Mechanical Engineering. My first choice, Drexel University in Philadelphia, had seemed out of reach. My school counselor had asked me to mix a couple of safe choices with the ones that were my first and second choices. At Drexel, I had requested a personal interview. I was selling myself hard. Four other colleges had already accepted me. I wanted to go to Drexel. In January, I got the letter I was hoping to get. Drexel said, "You are accepted." It was a combination of things: my Power-Point presentation to the admissions director, my sincere letters, my list of extra-curricular activities, and yes- my essay about my height and my dilemma with the surgery.

Then in November 2003, when we were preparing to go to London to attend my cousin Neha's wedding, Mom, Dad, and I saw a story on *60 Minutes* about this doctor in Texas who believed that hormone treatments should help any short person. This is not what we had heard from many doctors over the last ten years. This doctor, Dana Hardin, said on *60 Minutes*, "No one needs to be short." She talked about Eli Lilly's growth hormone, Humatrope, for healthy children who do produce the hormone but are still in the shortest 1.2 percent of their age group.

Dr. Hardin had an optimistic tone that was refreshing. Unfortunately, I was already seventeen. The window of opportunity had closed for me. Dad still called her office the next day. Her secretary said, "Since the airing of the story on *60 Minutes*, we have been getting hundreds of calls." Dad prepared a sincere letter with a plea to see us. Mom and Dad talked about what to do to get Dr. Hardin to notice our letter.

Dad said, "Let us first send a fruit basket to her office with a note saying, 'Please read my letter coming by FedEx tomorrow.' That way, their staff will be more likely to send our letter to the doctor." We do not know whether it was the fruit basket that did the trick, but Dr. Hardin did read our letter and sent us an e-mail the very next day. She said:

Dear Mr. Shukla, it is with great sadness I read your letter. I am so sorry that I did not meet your son earlier. I would be willing to see him if there is any possibility that I can help him. To know this, I will need a bone age x-ray. Could you please have his regular doctor obtain a bone age x-ray (left hand x-ray) and please Fed Ex to my academic office at 5323 Harry Hines Blvd. G2.226 Dallas 75390-9063. If your son's growth plates are not completely fused (I can know once I look at his bone age) then growth hormone may help him get some additional height....depends on how close to fusion. Please send me this x-ray and I will let you know if it is worth a try. I hope so.

Again, I am sorry not to have met him sooner.

Reading that letter, you could choose to be happy or sad. We decided to be happy. There was a glimmer of hope. Maybe the hormone treatment would work after all.

We sent the x-ray by FedEx. Dr. Hardin quickly wrote that the growth plates in the hand and wrist were fused but there was an off chance that the long bones were not completely fused. She said it was not likely to produce good results but if we wanted to, we could try the growth hormone treatment for three months.

What did we have to lose- money? Yes- about $5,000 for the first three months' supply of the prescription. If it worked, we would have to buy additional supplies. I would need to get a shot every day. There was no question who would give me the daily shots. My mom could learn to do these things within days. She hired a nurse, who came home one night and taught Mom how to give shots. The nurse brought with her an orange. She taught Mom how to stick a needle in an orange. From the next day on, Mom did the task expertly. She would have to give me the shots every day. I am no fan of taking a needle in the arm every day. It was still a more attractive option than the doctor taking a chisel and breaking your leg bone into two.

Three months went quickly. The needles were less painful than I thought. My height did not change even one-tenth of an inch. It was now March 2004. Only in November, we had felt new hope in our heart when we found a doctor who thought the hormone treatment should work for almost anybody. Dr. Hardin was kind and passionate. Unfortunately, it was way too late. If only we had known about Dr. Hardin a few years ago.

5 Second Visit to Dr. Paley

Now that the Hardin experiment had failed, we knew in our heart that the surgery was the only option left. I was not looking forward to the gruesome surgery, but I also knew that I did not want to be four feet eleven inches.

I had discussed the idea of surgery with my friends at school. Some of my teachers also knew about it. The reaction from most people was, "I did not know such a thing was possible." Mom and Dad were talking with many of our friends and relatives. There was hardly anyone giving enthusiastic support. The most common theme we heard was, "Accept what God has given to you." At times, Dad was getting annoyed at unsolicited advice. When one of his friends said, "Accept what God has given to you," Dad asked him why he colored his hair.

The friend said, "That is different."

"But God wanted you to be gray," said Dad.

At school, someone told me something similar. I understood their concern, but what they did not understand was how they were weakening my resolve.

In April, Mom made an appointment to see Dr. Paley. This time, we knew we would have to finalize everything. On May 6, 2004, once again we were on the New Jersey Turnpike, driving towards Balti-more. I said to Dad, "How tall do you think I will be after surgery?"

He said, "Paley said three inches. But if we take extraordinary care, I think you may be able to get three and a half inches out of this."

That would be good. I was fifty-nine-and-a-half inches. An additional three inches would make me five feet two-and-a-half inches. Then platform shoes could add another inch. I will be close to five feet four. Only a year ago, that sounded like an impossible dream.

We reached the hospital at twelve thirty p.m. The appointment was at one thirty. We were taken into the examination room at three thirty. A young Indian doctor came in at four p.m. He looked at the x-rays and said, "You are ready for surgery. The plates have fused. No more growth can be expected."

"Do you think we can do better than three inches?" I asked.

He said, "Who told you three inches? We only do two inches with ISKD."

Dad said, "Dr. Paley said two inches was a no-brainer; most patients get three inches."

"I don't think so," said the young doctor.

"Would we be able to talk to the patients who have done a similar surgery?" Mom asked.

"I don't think so," he said, and then left. We sat there, in deep confusion. We waited for another hour. Dad went and talked to a nurse and said, "Our appointment was at one thirty. It is now five. We have driven all the way from New Jersey. Can't you do anything?"

The nurse looked annoyed. She said, "People come to see Dr. Paley from a lot further. It is your choice whether you want to wait or not."

When Dr. Paley came in at five thirty, he did not even apologize. He said, "I can do the surgery in September."

I said, "Your associate said we can only get two inches."

"Yes, that is correct," said Dr. Paley.

"What happened?" Dad wanted to know.

"Well, we think that two inches makes sense," he said.

"But you had said three inches," Dad said.

"Well, what we do now is limit the lengthening to two inches, but we can do two surgeries. First, we can do it on the tibia and then, when we take the ISKD out from the tibia, we can also insert a new one in the femur. You will get a total of four inches. It will take about nine months. The hospital has agreed to do it as a special package price. So your total cost for both surgeries will be around $100,000."

Somehow, he did not sound very convincing. I knew Dad's antennas were going up. He asked, "Has something changed since we last saw you?"

"I think it is better to do two extensions of two inches. It is better."

"But what if all is going well? Would you not then let it go beyond two inches?" asked Dad.

"No. The device comes pre-configured to go only to two inches. There will be no chance to go more."

"What if we ask Orthofix to make a special device where you can decide whether to keep going after two inches?" Dad was trying every angle.

"No," Dr. Paley said in a resolute tone, "*I* do not do it over two inches. But I will do two surgeries and," he turned to me, "you can be four inches taller."

I liked the sound of it. I could be five feet three-and-a-half inches, then with platforms, almost my dad's height.

"Would it not be painful doing one surgery after another?" Mom wanted to know.

"No more than a single surgery," Dr Paley said in a matter-of-fact tone. He then said he would need a psychological evaluation quickly. Only after that could he schedule the surgery. "How is late August?" he asked.

When we left Baltimore, we were sad and excited at the same time. The single surgery had now become two surgeries, but a possible gain of three inches had changed to four. As we were getting on the turnpike, Dad said, "What are they not telling us?"

Mom and Dad were a lot more somber. Up until today, the surgery was a theoretical possibility. Now it had become real. The doctors would have to break my bones on both legs, between the knee and ankle. Then, just as it mended, they would do it to my upper leg.

During the last three years, every time I was losing my courage or Mom was getting nervous, Dad would say something to give us courage. That day, on the New Jersey Turnpike, Dad looked unsure. As we took Exit 9 for New Brunswick, he said, "I don't know." He shook his head and again said, "I don't know." After a few seconds, he said, "Akash, this is not a simple thing. A single surgery would be tough. How can we handle one right after other? It can tear a family apart. Even if you can handle it, I do not know whether our family can handle it."

Mom did not say anything. It was clear she agreed with Dad.

We came home. It was eleven p.m. I quickly changed. I then went to say goodnight to Mom and Dad. Dad was in his closet, changing into his night suit. I gave him a hug and said, "Dad, when I look at my life, I feel I am so very lucky. I have everything in life one can wish for and I have the best Mom and Dad in the world as my parents. I have only one regret, and that is my height. I know this will be a tough surgery. But I can handle it. Dad, if there is any family that can handle it, then it is us. We can do it, Dad!"

Dad started sobbing. Mom walked to us and put her arms around us. Three of us filled the closet space with our sobs.

We knew then that we had decided to go ahead with this gruesome surgery.

6   Encounter With a
       Psychologist

D r. Paley's office had given us the name of the doctor who would do
the psychological evaluation to decide if I was a good candidate for
the surgery. "Why do we need this Dad?" I asked.

Dad said, "This is not an easy surgery. They will break your legs
and insert a metal rod. If you then say, 'I change my mind,' there is
nothing anyone can do to get things back the way they were."

Mom and Dad started having long discussions with me every day to
make sure I fully understood what I was going to go through. I wasn't
too keen on the idea of going to see a shrink, but I had no choice. We
talked about how the evaluation was not necessarily to protect my inter-
ests, but to protect the doctor. That way, a patient cannot sue the doctor
and say, "You did not tell me how tough the surgery was."

Dr. Paley recommended a psychologist in Baltimore, Dr. Walter
Windisch, a PhD. Mom looked at the calendar. I would graduate high
school in the first week of June. She made an appointment with Dr.
Windisch for June 12, 2004. During that period, Dad kept saying he
did not like the way our meeting went with Dr. Paley. Mom and I
agreed. Dr. Paley seemed distant. He made no efforts to connect with
us. On top of that, the procedure was now limited to two inches.
Something must have changed with the procedure.

At his work, Dad asked Glenn Rupp to get more information about the ISKD. Glenn called the distributor for the manufacturer and asked if he would talk to my dad. In a conference call, Dad asked the distributor if the procedure was safe. The distributor said he knew nothing that would alarm him. Glenn asked him, "If it was your son, would you go ahead with this?"

"Yes I would," said the man. Glenn asked if he would send the actual ISKD rod for us to look at. As a professional courtesy from one orthopedic manufacturer to another, the distributor gladly agreed. A few days later, Dad called from work. "When can you and Mom come see Glenn to discuss the surgery?"

We went to Dad's company the next day.

Mom and I sat in Glenn's office. Glenn opened a case, about six inches wide and fourteen inches long. He took out the ISKD- the actual product. As I held it in my hands, Glenn went step by step and explained how the procedure would be done. With a reassuring smile, he turned to Mom and said, "I would not worry about this, Meena."

Mom was relieved. These words meant more to her than words from some of the doctors.

As a part of his job, Glenn Rupp routinely visited the Hospital for Special Surgery in New York. One of the top surgeons there had agreed to be on the advisory board for the new products for Dad's company. Dad asked Glenn if he could ask that doctor to recommend someone else. "I know Paley is number one in his field, but should we not consult at least one other doctor?" Dad asked me.

I told Dad, "Paley seems distant. I hope we can find a doctor who treats us with a bit more compassion."

Glenn got the name of a doctor in New York, a Dr. Rozbruch. He then sent him an e-mail, first talking as a manufacturer of orthopedic parts, and then saying, "Can you see our president's son?"

Dr. Rozbruch sent an e-mail the next day, "Yes, I would be glad to see them." We got an appointment for June 30.

In the meantime, the psychologist from Maryland, Dr. Windisch, contacted me by phone. He said, "I need to send you consent forms and other legal documents." When they arrived, I was surprised to see that most of them were about us promising him a prompt payment.

For our appointment in Baltimore for 12 June, we left New Jersey early in the morning of June 11 for Washington DC. We first drove around the DC area, visited the newly opened World War II memorial, and then drove to Baltimore in the evening. Mom had booked a nice suite at the Marriot Hotel, right on the harbor. She wanted to make sure we were in a "vacation" frame of mind. Deep down we knew we were moving closer to saying yes to a frightening experience. This was her way to make other things more pleasant.

In the evening, we walked around in the beautiful harbor area. I was acting happy but was nervous about meeting the shrink the next day. We had a lovely dinner at Amicci's, a quiet little Italian Restaurant.

The next morning, we drove to the address given by Dr. Windisch. As we entered the office building, we did not see his name on the list of doctors. Dr. Windisch came down to meet us in the reception area. We did not see a receptionist or many other patients. Dr. Windisch took us upstairs and then first met with my parents. He needed to know if the parents knew what they were getting into. It took him no time to realize that this family had done their homework. He asked many pointed questions. "What if there is a problem of non-union?" he asked. That would mean that after the lengthening was accomplished, the bone would not fuse together.

"Why do you ask this?" Dad asked, "Have there been many cases of non-union?"

"Only when they try to get too much lengthening," said the doctor. He then talked to Mom and Dad about the pain. He said, "You know that there is nothing in the world that prepares you for pain like this. Do you think Akash is ready? Do you think you are ready? The pain is more severe than an open heart surgery."

"You will tell all of that to Akash, won't you?" Dad asked.

"Yes, I will."

Dad and Mom were very reflective. They both said this was not an easy decision. Dad said, "The safest thing for us to do is to say no- we would be praised as cautious parents. But we are not looking for praise. We are not looking to avoid being blamed. We are looking for what is right for Akash and what will make him happy."

Dad later said that he could not figure out the motivation of Dr. Windisch. On one hand, he seemed to be saying, "Don't do it." On the other hand, he was saying, "Go right ahead."

After spending an hour with Mom and Dad, Dr. Windisch was ready for me. He asked Mom and Dad to leave us by ourselves. There was not a single other person in that three-story office building. "Come back at lunch time to pick up Akash for lunch, and then drop him off and come back at around seven p.m.," he said. That would mean I was going to get my money's worth. His fee for the single day's service was $2,200. He asked me to step into one of the offices.

First, he made me take tests on a computer. They were multiple-choice answers. I took three such tests, each taking about half an hour. Then, Dr. Windisch took me into another room and began a more formal interview. "Why do you want to be taller?"

"Being short has held me back in so many ways, both socially and physically," I said.

He said, "I want you to describe this surgery to me as if I was from another planet." I told him exactly what the procedure would be like. He seemed satisfied that I knew what I was getting into.

Next, Dr. Windisch showed me a bunch of pictures, and asked me to tell a story as to what happened before the picture, during the picture, and after the picture. I had no idea what this had to do with being prepared for the surgery. Most of the answers I gave had a romantic bend. Talking with my dad, Dr. Windisch had known that both Dad and his dad are writers. Dr. Windisch said, "I can tell you come from a family of writers."

Mom and Dad came to get me for lunch. After lunch, Mom and Dad went back to the hotel. They then took a long boat ride to keep themselves busy. At one point, the ride made a half hour stop. Mom and Dad got out for a walk on a deserted street. The street had rails for a tramway. Dad was staring at this strange scene- an empty road with rails in the middle, not a car or a single human being in sight, and an eerie silence. He held Mom's hand and shook his head.

"What is it, Rahul?" Mom asked in a concerned voice.

Dad said haltingly, "If thirty years ago someone had told us, 'You two will be married, will live in the USA, and will have a loving son, but he will be short. You two will take him for a pre-surgery evaluation to a city called Baltimore and while your son is cooped up with a shrink, you two will take a boat ride. You will get down on an empty street and will be walking on a road with the railroad tracks right in the middle of the road.'" Dad was staring blankly in the sky, his voice breaking down from the lumps in his throat. He was silent for a few seconds. Then he shook his head and said, "We would not have believed a word of that."

Mom looked at Dad and shook her head as if to say, "I know none of this feels real."

They went back to the hotel and then went for some snacks at a waterfront restaurant. When the waitress brought the food, Mom and Dad sat there staring at it. Then Dad said "Our friends, our family, no one knows what we are going through." His voice drowning in sorrow, he continued, "We need support, not advice." He covered his face with his hands and started weeping. Mom started sobbing. They held each other's hands and cried for several minutes. Then it was time for them to come pick me up.

Back at the doctor's office, the last thing I was doing was taking the inkblot test. The test took two-and-a-half hours. By the time we finished, it was seven at night. We both headed downstairs to meet my parents. I had spent six hours with this guy. I did not care anymore whether he was going to give an okay or not. At that time, all I wanted was to get the hell out of his office.

We were a bit quiet during the four-hour ride back to New Jersey. For the next few days, we kept discussing our experience with Doctor Windisch. His nearly empty office, very high fees, and the discussion about non-union had made us uncomfortable.

A few days later, he sent us an e-mail asking me to call him to discuss this matter by phone. He wrote that his fee did not include making long distance calls and he preferred that we call him. Wow! At ten cents a minute, if he talked to me for fifteen minutes, that would be a huge financial loss to him of one dollar and fifty cents. Our discomfort was on the rise.

I called him the same evening. He said he was having a tough time deciding whether or not I was ready for this surgery. He said, "What concerns me, Mr. Shukla, is you seem to be in a lot of emotional pain due to being short."

No shit, I thought to myself, otherwise why would I be subjecting myself to this painful freaking surgery?

Windisch said that because I was unhappy about my height and was almost in depression, I might not make a good candidate for such a tough surgery. I wanted to say, "If I was not unhappy about my height, I would not consider this surgery at all; in which case, I would never have needed to see you, you moron!"

I did not say anything, just listened.

Dr. Windisch then asked me if I was taking any anti-depressants. I told him no. He said he wanted to see me again and analyze me some more. "Only then may I give you a go-ahead for this surgery," he said.

I told him I'd think about it, and then reported to my parents what Dr. Windisch had said. We were puzzled. Maybe Dr. Windisch had a point, but we did not see it. And we decided that we had better keep looking for other options a little while longer.

7 Search for a New Surgeon

In two more weeks, we were scheduled to see Dr. Rozbruch at the Hospital for Special Surgery in New York. Dr. Paley in Baltimore was considered the number-one authority in the world for limb lengthening surgery, but it was still a good idea to get a second opinion.

On June 30, we left the house at about 8:40 a.m. My mom and dad were both a little tense. I was nervous and just ticked off. Why did I have to be so short? Now I had to go shop for a doctor from hospital to hospital. None of my friends had to do this. I had to go tell the doctors my life story, show them my height charts, and then plead with them to make me taller. Why couldn't I be happy with my height? I was thinking. Then I started dozing off.

Mom and Dad started yelling at me, "Why can't you read or something?" They would not shut up.

All of us were tense and irritable. What was the best way to get to 70th Street? Mom and Dad were arguing. Anything to do with the surgery was making us all uptight. The slightest difference of opinion was turning into a huge argument. Maybe Dad was right- this kind of surgery would indeed tear a family apart. We took the Lincoln Tunnel; then, from 42nd Street, we went east. The Hospital for Special Surgery was on 72nd Street. The doctor's office was also on 72nd Street. They had asked us first to go to another office on 72nd Street to get a full x-ray.

We were coming across unexpected one-way streets. Dad was angry with Mom. Mom was angry with me. I was angry with the person who designed the streets of New York and angry with God for making me so short. We finally got to 72nd Street. Dad parked the car, but then we could not readily find out where the x-ray lab was.

"Are you sure you understood them correctly?" Dad asked Mom. He sounded annoyed. Mom went from one office building to another until she found the right place. Ten minutes later, one of the attendants called me into the back room. The x-ray machine was huge, almost like an MRI machine. I had to lie down on a stretcher-like bed. The x-ray head was mounted on an eight feet long track.

Once they finished taking x-rays, we had to wait in the reception room for a few more minutes. Then the technician walked out with a two feet by three feet envelope in his hands. "Here are your x-rays," he said. This was their standard practice- take the x-ray, hand it to the patient, who then takes it to their doctor.

Dr. Rozbruch's office was on the same street, only two buildings away. The office was on the second floor. The receptionist seemed very pleasant. Within half an hour, I was taken into the examination room. A nurse came and checked my height. Then in a few minutes, Dr. Rozbruch came in. Dr. Rozbruch was a tall, fit man. His receding hairline made him look older than he was but also made him look seasoned. There was a pleasant sense of professionalism about him. He shook Dad's hand. Dad thanked him for agreeing to see us. Rozbruch turned to Mom, shook her hand, and then turned to me. "Hello Akash. Did I pronounce your name right?" He asked me to walk in the hallway.

"Why?" I asked.

He said, "I want to see how you walk *now*." He then asked me to lie down on the examination table and he bent each leg at the knee. His assistant was writing down the range of motion in each direction. Then the doctor held the bottom of my leg by the forefoot and ankle and flexed it in various directions to check the range of motion at the ankle. As I later found out, the normal position where the foot makes a ninety-degree angle with the leg is called neutral. Dorsiflexion is when the ankle moves towards body; plantarflexion is when it moves away from the body. The

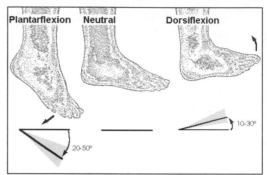

stretching of muscles during the lengthening process tends to pull the ankle away from leg. That would create a permanent disability. To prevent such disability, the patient needed to do vigorous exercise during the lengthening process to maintain the neutral position.

All in all, Dr. Rozbruch must have spent half an hour just measuring my joint movements. I was wondering why Dr. Paley or his associates never found it necessary to check the range of my joint motion. Once the examination part was over, the doctor sat next to me and started describing various options available to me. He said there were three possible approaches. The first was the ISKD. In this method, the entire device was inserted inside the tibia canal with no screws, bolts, or wires sticking out. He said there had been some problems with this method and it was not *his* preferred method.

"What kind of problems?" Dad asked.

"Well, sometimes non-union," said Dr. Rozbruch. Non-union was a serious problem. Once they cut your bone into two and then if your body refused to mend and fuse it back, what the hell would you do? Rozbruch said that it would be a serious complication but could be fixed with bone grafting.

Option number two was to use an external fixator, the very sight of which had given me chills in Doctor Paley's office in Baltimore. At that time I had said, "I would never, ever go through that kind of procedure." In that technique, a circular frame was placed around the leg below the knee. The frame was a circular external fixator, based on a hexapod system, consisting of two carbon fiber rings connected with

six telescopic struts. The rings were bolted into the bone, one right under the knee, another just above the ankle. Threaded screws went through your skin and into your bone. Some wires went right through the bone. The top and middle rings were connected by six telescoping struts.

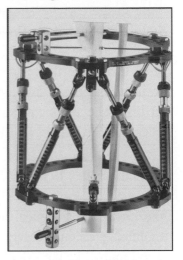

Once the rings were securely attached to each leg, the surgeon would break the bone. Once the patient was sent home, the patient would start moving each strut a certain amount. This would create a force that pushed the upper and lower rings apart. As a result, the bone that was broken would pull further apart. The body would start working on the normal healing process. A blood clot would be formed between the gap of the bone. Eventually and miraculously, the blood clot would become a new bone.

Doctor Rozbruch explained that the limb lengthening had been performed successfully for about fifty years. It started in Kurgan, Russia. Dr. Gavriil A. Ilizarov developed the concept in 1951 after seeing many WWII veterans who had leg fractures that had not healed (non-unions).

There is an interesting history about this procedure. Dr. Ilizarov first developed an external fixation frame to mend fractures. Knowing that compression of the fracture would help stimulate bone healing, he built a frame that had this capacity. He instructed a patient to gradually compress the non-union by turning a rod. However, the patient turned the rod the wrong way and caused distraction (separation) of the fracture. Ilizarov noticed that new bone had formed in the gap between the bone ends. That was the beginning of much research and development that showed that limb lengthening was possible, safe, and effective.

Ilizarov and his colleagues performed thousands of limb lengthening procedures in Kurgan, Russia. Russian politics, however, made education and communication with the Western world very difficult. Finally, Italian surgeons started performing and improving the procedure in the early 1980s and a large center soon developed in Lecco, Italy. The first limb lengthening case in the United States was performed in 1988. At first, there was much resistance and skepticism from the U.S. orthopedic community, but limb lengthening had proven to be a very powerful and effective procedure. Dr. Rozbruch said one of his associate doctors was none other than the daughter of the pioneer Russian doctor, Dr. Ilizarov himself.

The third method, Dr. Rozbruch said, was really a variation of the second method. In the second method, once the desired lengthening was achieved, the patient had to continue wearing the frame for months. In the third method, once the lengthening was achieved (in about three months), a second surgery was performed. At this time, an internal nail- a rod much like the ISKD- was inserted in the central canal of the bone that had just lengthened. The nail (rod) was locked in position by four screws, inserted from the outer surface of the leg into the IM rod. Only then would the frame be removed. Three months later, some of the screws would be removed. Nine months later, the nail itself was removed. In the third method, there were a total of four surgeries.

Dr. Rozbruch called this the "lengthening and then nailing" technique. He said he felt the first method was not a good idea because of possible non-union. In addition, my bone canal was not large enough to insert the ISKD. In that case, the doctor would have to ream the inner canal of my tibia bone to open up the inside diameter of the bone. That could be done, he said, but it also created a small possibility of permanently damaging the bone.

He said, "Go with the external fixator, but instead of doing it by method number two, go with the lengthening and nailing technique." He said it would be the most expensive option, but the safest and the one that allowed us the most flexibility. "With the external fixator, we can control the pace. If there is any problem, we can stop lengthening and then re-start. And we can go up to three inches- that is something we absolutely can't do with ISKD."

I said the idea of pins and wires sticking in my bone gave me chills. He said that it would only be for two months. Once I had the internal nail, I would not even know it was there.

"The only problem," he said, "is a possibility of infection of the nails, but you can control that by doing good daily pin cleaning."

By this time, the doctor had spent more than an hour with us. When he talked, he looked right into my eyes. He seemed to have a good sense of humor, and he seemed extremely bright. He also seemed much more pleasant than Dr. Paley.

As we were going home, Dad said that in his opinion, the ISKD and Dr. Paley did not seem like a viable option. "If we are not sure something is safe, we shouldn't even consider it," he said.

I knew he was right, but I was not yet ready to accept the idea of the external fixator with screws and bolts piercing into my legs. Suddenly, I did not want this surgery any more. That night, when I went to bed, I silently complained to God. The idea of ISKD was horrible enough. Now my family was leaning towards the external fixator. I prayed that a miracle would happen that night, and that when I woke up the next morning, I would be several inches taller.

I got up the next morning. A miracle had not happened. I was still short.

8 Why Not Write a Book About the Surgery

The next few days, Mom, Dad, and I had many more discussions about the procedure. None of us was thrilled about the external fixator. What a horrible sight! It had looked so very painful. During this time, at Dad's work, the Director of Quality, Carolyn Ketcham, had gone to attend a trade show for orthopedic surgeons. Upon her return, she said she had talked to someone there about ISKD. Carolyn said, "He expressed some concern."

Mom, Dad, and I sat down to discuss what we should do. Dad said, "Why don't we write a letter to Dr. Paley and ask him, point-blank, what has changed with ISKD?"

I said, "But we all like Dr. Rozbruch much better. Why not just walk away from Paley?"

Mom asked me, "Can you handle the external device?"

"I don't know," I said.

Dad said, "I'm sure there is nothing wrong with the ISKD, but the external fixator sounds like a better option." Mom nodded. I also knew that the ISKD was out. New York would be a more convenient location than Baltimore; the external fixator would give us the flexibility of controlling the pace of distraction. In addition, we did like Dr. Rozbruch a lot better. I took a deep breath and said, "I can handle the external fixator. But I am afraid about Dad. He will faint at the very sight."

Dad said, "I promise I will not faint." He said this with resolve. He has always used the quotation, "Mind over matter," but he is also famous for fainting at the sight of blood. I was not sure if he would be able to handle the sight of a fixator on my legs.

We had a follow-up appointment with Rozbruch's assistant, Dr. Svetlana Ilizarov. We drove to New York with a long list of questions. While waiting in the reception area, Mom started talking with a woman who had an external fixator on her left leg. The woman said she had been in a bad car accident. The fracture was so bad that part of the bone was crushed and broken off, making her lose about an inch of height on that leg. Since then, she had gone through four major surgeries. Each new surgery actually made matters worse. Then she heard of Dr. Rozbruch. Four months ago, she got the external fixator. The doctor was able to grow the bone by one inch; she was almost back to normal. Her voice full of gratitude, she said, "If it was not for Dr. Rozbruch, I would be limping for the rest of my life."

We were soon taken to the examination room. Dr. Ilizarov walked in a few minutes later. She was a slender woman in her thirties. She was pleasant yet quiet.

"What is the maximum distraction you have done?" I asked.

"Maybe three inches."

"Do you think I can achieve that?"

"Maybe you can but Dr. Rozbruch will tell you more about that."

Overall, we did not learn anything new but did come away with an impression that Dr. Rozbruch and his team knew their stuff. As we were leaving his office, Dr. Rozbruch's office manager, Omaira, gave us estimates on the cost of surgery. It would be a total of four surgeries. For the first phase of bolting the frames on each leg and fracturing the tibia bone, the hospital cost was estimated at $65,000. The second surgery would be three months later when the distraction was completed. At that time, the frames would be removed and a nail (rod) would be inserted from the knee down. The hospital cost for the second phase was estimated at $24,000. The third phase would be a minor ambulatory surgery where two of the screws that fastened the IM rod to the bone would be removed. The cost would be $4,000. On top of the hospital costs, the doctor's fees were estimated at $38,000 for all three surgeries. There would be a final surgery a year later when the rods would be removed. No estimate was given for that surgery.

Our minds were so focused on various medical details, I do not remember if we sat down to discuss the financial aspects at all. It wasn't that money was not an important issue, but we knew that we did not have much of a say in deciding how much we wanted to spend. Dad said he had loaned some $200,000 to his company. "We will use that money," he said.

The next day, we were visiting Dad's sister and her son, Asit (my cousin), his wife, Apexa, and their adorable daughters. Apexa told me her cousin, Nidhi, had gone through a similar procedure of lengthening one leg. It was done with an external fixator. "Wow, I would like to talk to her," I said.

"Well, it just so happens," she said, smiling, "Nidhi has come to see us. She is in the kitchen."

Nidhi, a pretty twenty-two-year-old girl, talked to me as if she had known me for a long time. She showed me where on her leg the frames were screwed in. She told me about the pain and said it was manageable. She loaned me a video tape on the fixator made by the manufacturer, Smith & Nephew. The tape showed how the frame was implanted on a patient's leg, how the struts would be adjusted to push the upper and lower frames apart, and how the pins and the screws holding the frame to the bone would need to be cleaned every day.

I forced myself to see the tape. The close-up scenes of how the frame was fixed on a person's legs looked gruesome. At one point, I thought I would throw up, but I was tired of being short. I had to do what I had to do. There were still times when I would lose my resolve. I told Mom how afraid I was.

One day, as we were all sitting at the dinner table, Dad said, "I can show you a way where you can get much more than just a few inches of height out of this experience."

"Well?" I was curious- what else could I get from the surgery?

Dad said, "It is going to be a very painful experience, like nothing you have ever experienced. Why not write a book on your experiences?"

I liked the idea. I had always enjoyed writing. I thought it would give me something to do with my pain. Dad said, "Look, not only will you be able to tell the world about your experience, you may make some money. Then you will have the proud feeling that you yourself have financed some of the medical expenses."

The real motivation Dad had was to change my frame of mind. Rather than thinking of myself as a victim, I would start thinking of myself as a scientific observer. They say, "If God gives you lemons, make lemonade." This would be an ideal example of that theory. My short stature had given me many heartbreaks. Now I was going to use it to create something positive in my life. After that point, whenever I told people about my intention of getting through the surgery, I would tell them in the next breath how I was going to write a book about my experience. Most people found it a fascinating idea.

It was a strange evolution. My mind was made up about writing the book; therefore, in a way, my mind was also made up about going ahead with this horrifying surgery. I only hoped that the surgery would go smoothly and that I would not have climactic chapters in my book.

9   One More Psychological Evaluation

Now that we were seriously considering having Dr. Rozbruch do the surgery, I would have to go through one more psychological evaluation. Dr. Rozbruch had asked that I be evaluated by a psychiatrist who they had been using. Her name was Dr. Ellen Westrich. By this time, we had already received the written evaluation by Dr. Windisch. He had said I may be a good candidate but that he needed to evaluate me some more before he could give his go-ahead. Our mind was more or less made up. Dr. Windisch and Dr. Paley were out; Dr. Rozbruch was in.

On July 12, Mom and I drove to New York to meet with Dr. Westrich. There was very light traffic on the New Jersey Turnpike. Once in Manhattan, the traffic was bad as usual. The doctor's office was on East 68th Street. We tried to go through the Central Park and got lost. After some frantic searching, we finally got to the right address. We were barely on time. Mom told me to get out and rush to her office, while she parked the car.

As I was climbing the stairs, I was feeling rotten inside. I did not want to see one more doctor to discuss my inner feelings about my height. I was also under tremendous pressure. What if I gave wrong answers and the doctor said I was not right for the surgery? What would I do then? I had already psyched myself up enough to skip the next year at Drexel. This surgery was going to be painful, but at least I would go to college several inches taller. What if suddenly I had to go to college in two months and accept my current height as my final height? That would suck!

Dad was an answer man. For almost any situation, he would give good guidance on how to give good answers. Not this time, though. I wanted to know what I should tell the doctor. He said, "Son, I have a dilemma. I think I know what the psychologist wants to hear, but I don't want to coach you with any answers. Nothing would be worse than to go through the surgery if you are not ready for it."

"Come on, Dad- help me out. What do you think they want to hear?" I pleaded. He would not budge, but I had figured out myself what the doctors wanted to hear. They wanted to make sure I knew what I was getting into. Secondly, they wanted to know if I had realistic expectations about this surgery. Of course I had realistic expectations. What other choice did I have? Was I happy with just two to three more inches? Fuck, no. But would I be less unhappy with those extra inches? The answer was yes.

As I was climbing the stairs, there was a lot of grimness and a lot of despair in my heart. Getting lost in Central Park had further pissed me off. But as I was climbing the stairs to Dr. Westrich's office, I said to myself, I'd better pull myself together and walk in with some positive energy. Otherwise, I would not do well in this evaluation. I needed to create some positive thoughts in my mind and then I remembered my conversation with Mom and Dad about a month ago.

At that time, Dad's cousin's son, a world-renowned surgeon from Tata Hospital in Bombay, was visiting us. Dr. Parool Shukla had performed some of the most complex surgeries for liver cancer. He frequently visited the USA to give talks, advise surgical manufacturers, and give speeches at USA universities. We had discussed this procedure with him. He is bright and levelheaded. He said, "What you are doing in this surgery is a controlled fracture. You are hoping that the fracture will mend correctly." There was caution in his tone. It was clear that he was suggesting not going ahead with the surgery. My own doctor, Bharti Shah, who I lovingly call "Dr. Auntie," was not too thrilled about the surgery, either.

Mom and Dad were consulting many experts and sharing their views with me. In the end, I still wanted to go ahead with it, but I was frightened at the same time. One day, Mom said, "Look, you have the right to change your mind until the very last minute."

I said, "I want to go through it." But then I started talking in rage about why God had done this to me. Why was I so unlucky? I started screaming.

Dad calmed me down. He said, "Akash, there are many short people in the world. They do not have the financial means to do anything about it. At least in our case, God has given us the means to do something about it. You are not that unlucky after all. You could have been just as short and without any options. At least here, it is your decision."

That was right. That was exactly what I had said in my college essay. So climbing the stairs to Dr. Westrich's office, I reminded myself as to how fortunate I was. It put a smile on my face. I opened the door. I was ready to see the doctor.

I entered into a small but well-decorated office. Dr. Westrich met me in the reception area. She greeted me with a warm handshake. She led me to the back room, and told me to sit down on her couch. I was still a bit nervous, and jokingly said, "I never thought that I'd have to sit on a psychologist's couch at this young age."

Dr. Westrich started with, "Let me tell you what we are going to do today." She told me that first she would be asking me questions. "You can tell me why you want this surgery done." She said that she'd have me draw some pictures.

Draw pictures? I really suck at that, I thought. I said, "That's fine. I just hope that the artistic quality of the drawings doesn't affect your decision about whether I am ready for the surgery or not."

"No, it will not," she smiled. The last thing, she said, would be the inkblot test. I told her I had gone through that only a few weeks ago.

Once Mom got in, they talked for a while, and then Mom waited outside. The doctor started with the usual first question: "Why do you want this surgery?" What she was really asking was, "Why would you put yourself through such extreme pain, both emotional and physical, all for a small increase in height of two inches?"

I started telling her stories of how my short stature had caused problems in my life, mainly social. I was afraid to approach girls I liked because they always thought I was younger than I was. I had to dress older. The list went on and on. I then said, "Dr. Westrich, I know that with this surgery, I'll still be short, but I won't be apologetically short." That was an interesting phrase. I think she understood what I meant. I used it several times again that day.

Next, she asked me to draw a picture of a man. I thought for a while, and in my amateurish manner, drew a picture of a man with a mustache and beard. Next, Dr. Westrich asked me to draw a picture of a woman. I drew a thin, curvy woman, wearing a skirt. She was much shorter than the man. Next, she asked to draw a family. She noted that in all my pictures, men were much taller than women. Dr. Westrich asked me how tall I wanted to be. I explained that I knew this surgery wouldn't make me tall, but it would make me less short. It would get me close to the average height of a woman in the USA and taller than the average height of an Indian woman.

The last thing we did was the inkblot. Then it was over. She was professional, pleasant, and to the point. Her fee was one-fourth of what we paid to Windisch. In a few days, we got the written report. It had several sections. In Behavioral Observations, the doctor noted, "Mr. Shukla was initially trepidatious and did not make eye contact but became more engaged as the evaluation progressed." She noted that my "speech was normal, thinking was coherent and goal directed," and that I "did not show any evidence of suicidal or homicidal behavior." I chuckled reading that paragraph and said to Dad that maybe this was a compliment!

Under the paragraph called "IPAT: Beck Depression Inventory," she noted that I showed "statistically significant items to indicate depression." I knew that the last few years were pretty tough for me. Reading the report from the doctor, I realized that things must have been a lot tougher than I had thought. She noted that I showed evidence of considerable emotional stress. She then stated, "He demonstrates good abilities to perceive the world conventionally to form accurate information."

Thank God, I thought.

In the summary paragraph, the doctor stated, "Mr. Shukla presents a pleasant young man who clearly experiences much distress about his body, notably his stature." She added, "He expresses realistic expectations of what the surgery can and cannot do for him." She did not clearly say in the report whether I was a good candidate for the surgery but I surmised that I was.

During that period, I had kept in close touch with my extended family, cousins, uncles, and aunts. They were all telling me that I was very brave to want to go through this surgery. One cousin, Meetali, who got married only a few months earlier had told me, "If you ever need to talk about anything at all- I don't care what time it is- call me." That meant a lot to me.

In the last week of August, the phone rang. I picked it up. It was Dr. Rozbruch's office. The woman on the other end said, "Dr. Westrich gave the go-ahead. When do you want to schedule the surgery? Your Mom had said the eighteenth. Is that okay?"

I heard the words but did not fully process their meaning. I said, "Yes, September 18 is fine," and hung up the phone. Dad was at work; Mom had gone to see Dad's parents at my uncle's place. I slowly walked away from the phone. This was it. All the philosophical discussion was coming to the end. The great dilemma of whether the surgery was a good idea or not would become a moot point.

I slowly walked into the family room. My knees were buckling. I collapsed on the sofa. I was breathing hard and heavy. I knew there was no more turning back. I picked up the phone and called Meetali. I got her answering machine. I left a message, saying that the date for the surgery had been fixed and that I was scared shitless. She called me in the evening. I talked to Cousin Meetali and her husband for an hour.

Mom and Dad were very quiet that night. The journey to find the solution to my unsolvable problem was coming to an end. The next journey- the actual limb lengthening- was about to begin.

10 The Surgery Date
Is Approaching

D ad's parents were visiting from India. Grandma said, "We will not be able to see Akash go through the surgery." They pleaded with us to let them go back to India prior to the surgery. Dad's company had an Open-House for all the employees on September 19. We therefore changed the surgery date from Saturday, September 18, to Friday, September 24. Grandma and Grandpa left for India on September 18.

As the surgery date approached, the level of activity in the house was picking up at a feverish pace. On the eighteenth and nineteenth, Mom was on the phone, placing an order for many things. A Tempurpedic bed was ordered. This bed had a mattress made of special material. It would form into the shape of your body. It also had motorized adjustments. At $1,500, it wasn't cheap. It was delivered on Monday, September 20. Mom was busy making special clothes for me, such as pants that could fit over the frames. She purchased a hospital-style rolling table and support rails for the toilet.

Mom and I made numerous trips to the local surgical supplies store- Williams Surgical in Plainfield, New Jersey. We placed an order for a wheelchair. Should we buy it or rent it? We decided to rent it at $80 per month. We knew that going in and out of the house and into the garage wouldn't be easy. We needed to take measurements as to how many feet of a drop it was from the hallway down to the garage. That would determine how long a ramp was needed. We gave the information to Williams Surgical. Mom was an expert executor. Her skills were coming in handy in preparing for the surgery.

On September 20, the wheelchair came in. Strangely, I was excited about the courageous journey I was about to embark upon. When Dad came home from work, I could not wait to show him how I would move around in the wheelchair. My new room was shaping up. It was the room that, until the previous day, was used by our housekeeper who by now had become a family member and I even called her "Auntie".

The Tempurpedic bed was in place, and the wheelchair was in. On the evening of September 20, I was almost giddy and started practicing how I would transfer from the wheelchair into the bed. Dad, while taking a movie of the practice maneuvers, kept joking that the transfer was a lot easier and lot more fun while the frames were not drilled and screwed into my legs.

I said that my wheelchair would make my arm muscles stronger. I then looked at Dad with a sad twinkle in my eyes. "Dad, it feels weird to say *my wheelchair*." The fake festivity was giving in to the sad realization that my life was going to go though some drastic ups and downs.

On Tuesday, September 21, we had to go for pre-admission procedures at the hospital. They were going to do a lot of tests on me to verify that I was ready for the surgery. I also needed to see Dr. MacKenzie. He was going to be the general physician during the surgery.

Dr. MacKenzie was a compassionate and an enlightened man. He taught medical ethics at Cornell University. He told me not to worry and that all would go well. I told him about my dilemma about whether this was the right thing. I told him about my college essay, titled, "To Change the Things I Can." He asked for a copy of the article. When I later e-mailed it to him, he sent me a very warm reply.

From the hospital, we then stopped by the building right across from the hospital. It was connected to the hospital by a walkway bridge across the street. The place was called Bel-Air. It had several one bedroom and two bedroom apartments that the patients' families could rent. In a way, it was like a hotel except that it was the part of the hospital. Mom had booked a regular size unit at $180 per night. We decided to upgrade it and asked for a larger unit. Based on what we were told by Dr. Rozbruch's office, we expected to stay in New York for four days. The doctor had suggested that he might discharge me even in three days if I was coming along okay. We would only find out later what a pipe dream that was.

Wednesday, September 22, was the last full day at home before the surgery. The anxiety was setting in on Mom and Dad. There was no turning back anymore. Dad said to Mom, "We take a kid in perfect health to the hospital. They break the bone in his leg into two and drill holes in his leg bone. How does that make sense?"

September 22 was also the day when Dad had to fast. That meant that he could only have fruits and liquids. Why? Because a debt to God had to be settled. Dad is not a religious person. He is philosophical, writes articles about the existence of God, but does not believe in any of the superstitious procedures - except when it comes to his parents and his son.

Two years ago, I had joined the wrestling team. Week after week, I was losing every single match. Mom and Dad came to every one of my wrestling matches and knew how much I was looking for my first win. Then one day, when Mom was already at the school gym, Dad left work early and sat next to Mom. They were hoping for my win but expected that this match would go just the way all the others had gone.

But that day, I was doing surprisingly well. The kid was a little taller than me but from the first moment, I somehow felt an emotional upper hand. The partisan crowd was screaming, *"Go Akash- Go Akash."* Suddenly, it appeared that I could *win* this one.

Dad quickly became religious and started silent negotiations with God. He said, "Oh God, let Akash have his first win. He deserves it."

And then, as they used to do it in the India of the 1950s, Dad promised God, "If Akash wins, I will fast for one whole day."

Well, what do you know? The next minute, I pinned the guy. That night, Dad told me he owed one hungry day to God. Mom had also promised a few things to God. We all laughed at this. Two years went by and Dad never got around to fasting. God had the whole universe to run. We were sure he/she probably forgot all about it. But then came the date for the surgery. Dad, an otherwise logical person, was not going to take a chance with the almighty God, so he said, "Let me fast on September 22 and get this out of the way."

Mom, who ordinarily would talk Dad out of any promise that required him not to eat, was not arguing at all. It was one thing to break a promise to some ordinary Tom, Dick, or Harry, but you do not fool around with God. Mom wanted Dad to pay up the debt.

As Dad later told me, at work he had to attend several meetings. The meeting about a new India plant was supposed to last for half an hour and it lasted two hours. During the first hour, Dad disagreed with everybody on everything. If they said, "We needed more machines in India," Dad said, "No, we need fewer machines." If they said, "Yes, fewer machines will do," Dad would get angry and say, "And then how would we meet the increased demand from other customers in the USA?" Suddenly Dad realized he was way too nervous about my surgery. And that was the reason why he was confrontational with everyone. He left at three and came home.

I was eating when he came home. He sat down with me and had fruits, which were allowed under the fasting rules for Indian gods. I said to Dad, "Can we go buy bicycle gloves so that I can wear them while pushing the wheels on the wheelchair?"

Dad told me how he thought I would be a lot more nervous than I was. In fact, I was not nervous at all. Part of me was excited. I was going to embark on this impossible dream. Everyone was telling me how courageous I was to have the balls to go through with this. Well, I was not nervous. That was a bit naïve, and I am glad I was that way.

Dad and I got in the car for our last shopping spree for that year. First, we went to Plainfield, to Williams Surgical. There we had to pick up the huge ramp. The ramp was about eight feet long, about four feet wide, and would fold in to half both lengthwise and widthwise. The rental was $80 per month.

Next, we went to a bicycle supply store. I looked at two different styles of gloves and bought both. There were enough things making us anxious. It wasn't worth it to agonize over which pair of gloves was better than the other.

Then we went to Costco and looked at a high definition large screen TV. We did not need another large screen TV, but Dad wanted to create a little more excitement for me when I came back from the surgery. That way, my post-surgery pain would become a little more tolerable. The TV at Costco was very reasonable- $1,100, not bad for a fifty-two inch HDTV. Dad and I were enjoying this one last day of shopping together. We knew it would be months- close to a year- before the two of us could be running around from shop to shop like this.

Mom was busy making arrangements for our travel to New York and giving final touches to my "recovery room." That night, Dad's brother, Uncle Rajen; his wife, Neha; their daughter, Juhee; Dad's sister, Rekha; her son, Asit; his wife, Apexa; and their kids, Ria, Reshma and Roshni came to see me and cheer me up. Dad turned on the camcorder and asked me, "Why are you going through this surgery?"

I said, "I am tired of what others think of me. Also, the average height of a woman is five feet three inches. I am four feet eleven-and-a-half inches. How would a woman feel dating me? If I am five-two and with proper shoes look five-four, then I am all set."

Dad said, "So all this pain is for the babes."

"You got it, Dad," I said. Then I said to Mom, "I feel okay now, but when I think of being at the hospital and the nurse comes to take me to the OR and says, 'Who is Akash Shukla,' that very thought makes my heart sink." Mom gave me a hug. "Everything will be fine," she said with loving conviction.

That night, as we went upstairs, we followed our standard routine. Ever since Dad started taking Zocor in 2003, he would complain of aching feet. So every night, when I went to say "goodnight" to them, I would sit on their bed and give a quick foot massage to Dad. During that time, we would turn on the TV, tune to channel eleven, and watch reruns of *Friends*. That had become a ritual with us. On September 22, we did all of that- but this time, we took a movie of our ritual. Then, as I walked to my room that night, Dad again took my movie.

I said, "It will be months before I will be able to walk to my room." I think Mom, Dad, and I were making a big deal about all of this just so that it would really sink in that life would be very different after tomorrow.

In retrospect, I am glad we made all that fuss to mentally prepare us. If we had not, what followed would have emotionally wiped us out.

11   We Leave for the Hospital

On September 23, Dad left for work, and Mom was on the phone making last minute arrangements. I was somewhat numb. Mom called the Hindu temple to find out when they would close. She called Dad at work and told him that the temple closed at eleven thirty a.m. and that Mom, Sushi Auntie, and I would meet Dad at the temple at ten forty-five.

Of course, we had to go to the temple before we left for the surgery. We were not going to go for surgery of this magnitude unless we first had a face-to-face with the supreme commander of the universe. Dad told Mom that from the temple, she could go to Costco to pick up the new TV. He said he would send two people from work with the company van to load and deliver the TV to our home.

By the time Dad reached the temple, it was 10:55 a.m. He was late, he thought. But Mom and I did not get there until eleven. Until then, Dad stood there quietly in the terrace of the temple. It was a pleasant fall morning, with bright skies and a cool breeze. "God, are we doing the right thing?" He was quietly communicating with God. Somehow, nothing seemed real at that time. Was all of this really happening? Was he really standing outside the temple?

Dad was thinking, "Akash and Meena will get here soon. Then we will drive to New York this afternoon, check into the hotel, go to bed, get up the next morning, and walk with Akash across the street to the Hospital for Special Surgery. There they will take him to the OR and cut his leg bone- both legs- into two pieces. Oh my God. Is this really happening or am I in some sort of hallucination?"

Our car was approaching the temple parking lot. There were no other cars in the huge parking lot. We got out. Dad walked down from the terrace and came to the car. We all somberly climbed the steps. We stopped at the temple clerk's office to purchase the "Archna," a packet of flowers, fruits, and other holy items, for nine dollars. "Archna," in Sanskrit, means "worship" or "request." When you take that Archna to the priest, he then asks your name, walks into the small room with the statue of God, and says a personal prayer to God, using your name in the prayer.

Mom quickly called Dad's sister to inquire about the sub-caste we belonged to. Dad was raised never to believe in caste and other Hindu religion traditions. He therefore did not even remember what sub-caste of Brahmin caste his family belonged to. But at the temple, the priest asks your sub-caste before he starts saying his prayers on your behalf. We did not want our prayers to not reach God on some minor technicalities. Our sub-caste- the "gotra," as it is called- was "Darlabh," said Rekha Auntie.

The temple in Bridgewater was a serene place. The main temple hall was a huge room, probably one hundred feet by one hundred feet, with marble floors and small shrines for individual gods. The Hindu religion does not have a single God Almighty but an organizational structure. You can choose to worship whichever god in that complex chain. At the top of the pyramid of hierarchy are three main gods: Brahma, the god in charge of creating and re-creating the universe, Vishnu, the god who takes care of running the day-to-day affairs for the universe, and Shiva, who is in charge of destroying the universe every couple of billion years.

Then there is Rama, the god who killed the evil king Rawan, Krishna, a very complex god who put his philosophical wisdom in the book of Geeta, Laxmi, the goddess of wealth, and Sarsvati, the goddess of knowledge. There are also nine small statutes of nine planet gods. For those nine gods, the ritual for the devotees would be to make nine complete circles around the podium with the statues of the nine planet gods.

We first went to that temple five years ago, when it first opened. Since then, we would visit the temple once or twice a year. Every time we went there, Dad and I would walk around the podium with the nine planet gods. He would tell me to keep the count. After every turn, I would raise my hands and show him with my fingers the current count. It was our own little ritual.

At the center of the hall, there was the main section of the temple with a large statue of Lord Venkateswara. This god is worshipped widely in southern India. Dad said he had never heard of this god when he was growing up, but in his heart, he always understood that in the name of God, we seek a divine intervention. All we are doing is accepting that by ourselves, we are not all that powerful and cannot always control the situations facing us. A god from south India would be just as helpful as some of our local gods.

We were the only four people in that large temple hall. The priest saw us walk to the statue of Lord Venkateswara. He saw the small plate of fruits and flowers in our hand. He knew we were there for Archna, a plea to God. The priest walked to us. We were standing five feet from the main shrine. Only the priest could walk inside that shrine. We could see the statue from standing outside. The priest looked at Mom and asked, "What is your name?"

Mom turned to me. I whispered, "Akash."

The priest then asked the gotra. Mom said "*Darlabh.*" The priest took our Archna with him, walked inside the shrine, and started saying his prayer in Sanskrit. Dad later told me that he closed his eyes and said only one sentence: "God, please look after my son." He did not want to complicate his request with any additional words. Mom had folded her hands together with her fingers touching her lips, her eyes closed. When she opened her eyes and looked at me, she saw, for the first time, a frightened look on my face.

The priest walked back from the shrine with a round metal jar in his hand. He put the jar on my head. Dad looked reassured. Somehow, it seemed to him that God had agreed to protect their son. Suddenly my eyes were filling up with tears. The peaceful quiet in the house of God was making me realize what lay ahead. I turned to Mom, put my head on her shoulder, and started sobbing. "I am so afraid," I said.

Mom hugged me. She could not say a word; tears were flowing from her eyes. Sushi Auntie was wiping her eyes. The priest looked at our sad faces. He did not say anything but figured out that this family was going through some serious crisis. Dad was staring at the statue of Lord Venkateswara and holding back tears. He hugged me, looked me in the eyes, and said, "I know everything is going to be okay."

I had always believed Dad. If he said he would take care of something, I knew it would be taken care of. Indeed, his confident words created comfort in me. I do not think they created much comfort in Dad, though. He knew that from that point on, we could do everything right but God would decide whether we would have a success or a horrible disaster in our hands.

We left the temple at eleven thirty. Mom went to Costco; Dad dropped me and Sushi Auntie at home and went back to work. The TV would not fit in the huge company van. Mom called Ziggy; he had finished our basement and did such a good job that Dad hired him in his factory. Ziggy had a truck. He went to Costco and then they delivered the TV at home.

By two p.m., Dad came home from work. Mom went to drop our dog, Genie, at the kennel. We needed to leave by four p.m. The Indian consulate in New York had sent Dad an invitation for a dinner reception that evening, a reception with the prime minster of India. If we left in time, reached New York at a decent hour, and checked in quickly, then Mom and Dad could go attend that reception. Dad knew it was an honor to be invited to such a reception, but more importantly, it had created a welcome diversion in our minds and gave us something else to think about rather than worrying about the events of tomorrow.

But at four p.m., we were still home. It was not likely that Mom and Dad would make it to the reception. At 4:10, we all went into our own "God" room, the room where we kept some pictures and very small statues of some gods. This same room would become my "recovery room" upon my return from the hospital. Mom, Dad, Auntie, and I stood in front of the small table. Mom asked me to light the lamp. We all then said our silent prayers, went to the garage, and got into my Jeep.

On our way to New York, the traffic was bad. Mom and Dad kept talking about how they were not going to make it in time to the Waldorf Astoria Hotel for the reception for the prime minister of India. Ordinarily, Dad would get all jumpy and anxious if we were late getting somewhere. Not that day, though. He said to Mom not to worry and said, "If we make it, we make it; if we can't, we can't."

Once in Manhattan, we again were caught in bad traffic on First Avenue. Overall, it took us two hours to get to the hotel. Once we reached it, Mom and Dad changed quickly and rushed to Waldorf Astoria. They were not late after all. They went through several security checkpoints and then to a huge reception room. There were some four hundred guests. In a few minutes, the prime minister of India entered the room. He gave a humble and thoughtful speech. When Dad came to the United States thirty-four years ago, he came as a penniless student and did not think that someday he would be invited to a private reception for the prime minister of India.

Heady stuff!

But more importantly, this was a very useful diversion. Not many other things could have taken their minds off of the worrisome surgery next morning. We could not have arranged, by ourselves, a reception with the prime minister of India on the eve of the surgery.

Maybe God did accept our "Archna" and was already looking after us.

12　The Day They Cut My Leg Bones in Two

Next morning, the alarm went off at five thirty a.m. I had a good night's sleep, but my mom and dad spent all night tossing and turning. At six fifteen, just as we were getting ready to leave the room, Mom lit a candle in front of a statue of God that we had brought with us. Mom, Dad, Auntie, and I stood there in silence.

As we crossed the street to get to the main hospital building, Dad stayed a few steps back and took a movie of us walking into the hospital. We took the elevator to the fourth floor to the admissions office. The admissions clerk was a middle-aged woman. She asked me what procedure I was to undergo. I said, "Bi-lateral limb-lengthening surgery."

"What do you mean?" she asked.

"I want to become taller so that I can date taller babes," I said with a chuckle.

"I didn't know they could do that," she exclaimed. "How much height are you hoping to gain?"

"Two to three inches," I replied.

She turned around and told a co-worker, with a look of disbelief, "Hey Charlie, this young man is going through surgery to make himself taller." Then she turned back to me and said, "Good luck and God bless you." Then it was down to business for her. She said, "You are not covered by insurance for this surgery. We need at least 30 percent now. How are you going to pay?"

Dad handed her his American Express card and paid $30,000 as an initial payment for the hospital stay. We had already made a payment of $12,000 to Dr. Rozbruch for his services.

From the admissions office, they directed us to the atrium on the same floor. The atrium had a glass wall facing the East River. It had high ceilings. It was big enough to seat at least seventy-five people. As soon as we entered the room, I saw my Uncle Rajen; his wife, Neha Auntie; Dad's sister, Rekha Auntie; her son, Asit; and his wife, Apexa. Also, Glenn Rupp from my dad's work was there. He had received special permission to be in the operating theater during my surgery. This was a great relief for everyone in my family, but especially to me. I knew there would be at least one familiar face in the operating theater.

Just as I was shaking hands with Glenn, a male nurse entered the atrium and announced my name. I looked at Dad's face. He and Mom looked a little stunned. I think things were happening a little too fast for them. Mom, Dad, and I walked into the pre-operative room. There were two beds. They put me in the one closer to the door.

I quickly changed into a hospital gown and climbed into the hospital bed. It felt very awkward to be lying in a hospital bed, especially because there was nothing wrong with me- yet. To my right, I could see the East River. It was a scenic morning. Were it not for the fact that I was soon going to get my body parts cut by sharp tools, I would have enjoyed this moment even more. I was feeling very nervous. Dad sensed that and asked me, "How are you doing?"

I tried to cover up my nervousness by saying, in a Chandler-like fashion (from *Friends*), "Could I *be* looking any cooler in this gown?" Everybody laughed.

Dad and I had talked about writing this book to create a diversion. I could fool myself into acting like a reporter, instead of being the recipient of all the pain and suffering. In the pre-op room, I felt that now was the time to go into reporter's mode. I asked Dad to hand me my journal so I could start writing. As I was writing, Dr. MacKenzie entered the room. He said he had given my essay to his two sons to read. He then said, "I have just come to wish you good luck. Don't worry; everything is going to be all right. I'll see you every day that you're here. Just hang in there." He then shook my hand. I felt a lot of warmth and feelings in his handshake. He was a good doctor, a good man, and goodness was written all over his face.

The level of anxiety in the room was steadily increasing. Just then, Dr. Arkady Blyakher came in. He asked me to stand up. He had a camera and he took my picture. I guess he wanted my pre-operative picture with my pre-surgery height. Almost an hour had passed in the pre-op room when a nurse came and said, "It's time to insert the IV" I complimented her on her stunningly good looks. She said, "That is all well and good but I still have to insert this IV in your hand." As the procedure began, I was squeezing the hell out of Mom's hand. She was stroking my hair.

By 8:20 a.m., two nurses came into the room and told me that they were going to shave my legs. The thought of two women shaving my legs was not pleasant. To hide my nervousness, I started making jokes about the whole situation. I said, "The only reason I'm doing this is so that I can date taller women."

They first applied a yellow substance, probably iodine, all over my legs. Then, with a razor, they began to shave my legs completely bald from the knee to the ankle. The fact that they were doing work on the legs made me realize that this is where all the cutting and drilling was going to be done. Just as the nurses finished, Dr. Rozbruch came into the room. He asked me if I was ready to go. I said, "I'm as ready as I'll ever be, Doc."

He said, "Don't worry about a thing, Akash. Everything is going to go just fine." He then wrote his initials on both of my legs with a permanent marker. This is a standard hospital procedure to prevent surgeons from operating on the wrong leg. That wasn't going to be a problem for me, since both of my legs were going to be operated on. Dr. Rozbruch gave a reassuring smile to my parents and said again, "Everything is going to be all right. Don't worry." He then turned to me and said, "I'll see you in the operating room."

At 8:50, they came to take me to the OR. I was still in a jovial mood. I was doing my best to keep my parents' spirits up and reassuring them not to worry. Mom and Dad held my hand and walked a few steps with my stretcher. Then Mom continued walking a few more steps while Dad turned on the camcorder. Yes, every step of the surgery was going to be recorded on the video tape!

As I got closer to the OR, I commented on how cold it was in the OR. Once I was in the O.R. I was surrounded by six or seven people who were going to assist the surgeons during my surgery. The anesthesiologist came and injected the serum into the IV. It burned like hell. In their blue gowns, all the people in the OR looked kind of dorky and I complimented them on their strong fashion statements. Then I fell into a deep sleep.

The whole while, my parents were anxiously waiting in the atrium. The first report they got on the surgery came at 12:20 p.m., from Glenn Rupp, who told my mom and dad how everything went without a glitch. While Glenn was still talking to Mom and Dad, Dr. Rozbruch came out and said, "Mr. and Mrs. Shukla, everything has gone very well. Akash is in the recovery room and you'll be able to see him soon."

When I opened my eyes, I asked the nurse, "What happened about my surgery?"

She said, "Your surgery is over."

I was surprised to hear that. I didn't even remember the surgery having started. Mom was the first person to come and see me. Mom was worried about how much pain I was in. I was so drugged up and numb that I did not feel much pain. Mom left and sent Dad. Only one person at a time was allowed to come inside the recovery room. Dad came in and whispered in my ear, "According to Dr. Rozbruch, the surgery went according to plan." Then, one by one, all my other relatives came to see me. I was falling in and out of sleep.

They kept me in the recovery room until five thirty p.m. Then two female nurses came to take me to my room on the fifth floor. As they were navigating my stretcher through the turns in the hallway, I said, "Do you want to hear a good joke?"

"Sure," they replied.

"There was a woman standing at a wishing well. She made a wish saying, 'I wish I had better driving abilities,' and as soon as she dropped the coin into the water, she turned into a man."

They started laughing. One of them said, "Listen, wise guy, don't forget you have two women drivers driving this stretcher."

They got me to the room. Mom and Dad were already there. One of the nurses said, "Your son is quite a comedian." My parents were happy to hear that- not because of my comedic skills, but it meant that I was doing okay.

By six-thirty, the pain was settling in. I could not move my legs. There was heavy hardware bolted and pinned to my bone. When I tried to look under the sheet, I saw my legs, covered in gauze. My body was drained. The legs, hips, and back were hurting. Why am I going through this? I was wondering. Why is it important to be a couple of inches taller? I slowly turned my head to Dad, motioned my dad to come closer, and said, "All of this because of the crap I got from the kids in my high school."

"Oh no, Son," Dad shook his head and said in a soothing voice, "They mean nothing, absolutely nothing. You're doing this because *you* wanted to do it." I nodded in agreement and then fell asleep.

I woke up again at about nine thirty. The pain was so severe, I could not figure out which part of my body was hurting. Mom and Dad looked in a state of utter disbelief. At ten, Dad was leaving for the night. Mom went with him for a quick cup of tea, but was going to come back and stay with me a little while longer. They walked across the street to their room. Mom had a cup of tea in her hand. She looked at Dad. Her lips were quivering, hands shaking. She put the cup down and said in a whispering tone, "Akash is in so much pain."

Dad pulled her head on his shoulder and Mom cried uncontrolla-ble, loud, wet sobs. The anxiety, built over the whole day, had to get out. She quickly composed herself and came back to the room. She said to me, "I will stay here until they throw me out."

By this time, I was extremely tired and barely could keep my eyes open. At eleven, Mom picked up the phone, called Dad, and said, "They haven't asked me to leave yet. I'm going to stay here as long as I can." By midnight, another nurse came in and told Mom that the sofa next to my bed opened into a very narrow, uncomfortable bed. The nurse got Mom a few blankets, and Mom was able to stay in my room all night. I slept well most of the night.

I woke up at six a.m. Mom started telling me how well the surgery went. I wanted to talk to Dad right away. I asked Mom to call Dad and ask him to come soon. Dad came in ten minutes. I told him in a raspy voice how, at night, the IV wasn't working properly and that I was in extreme pain. I showed him the dispenser button, and said, "When the pain becomes too much, I can push the button." If you had heard me that morning, you would have known that the realization had set into me about the severity of this surgery.

Once Dad came in, Mom went to their room to get ready. Then, while Dad and I were talking about an episode of *Friends*, I asked for the vomit tray and threw up. I was on the liquid-only diet and so a lot of liquid came out. Half an hour later, the breakfast delivery woman came in. She gave me two menus and a pencil. She said, "One is for you, and one is for your Dad." As I was looking at the menu, I asked Dad for the vomit tray and threw up again. The breakfast lady looked at me with sympathetic eyes, took back one menu, and said, "Honey, I know you won't want breakfast this morning."

She brought me ginger ale. I could barely take two sips. Half an hour later, I threw up again. Just then, Dr. MacKenzie came in. He said, "The pain killers do this to your stomach. All of this will settle down, probably by the evening." Dr. MacKenzie said, "Everything has gone exactly as expected." He had an encouraging smile on his face. Looking at his cheery face, I was already feeling a little better.

Dad gave me a quick sponge bath, and then forced himself to look at the dressings on my legs. From my ankle to my knee, I had ten-inch diameter rings, completely covered with dressings. This made each of my legs look bigger than twelve inches in diameter. As Dad had later told me, he started asking himself, "Is this pain worth it?" At that very moment, to him, the answer seemed to be "no." Then Dad left me 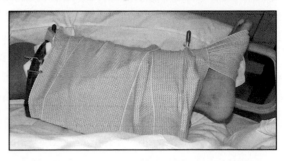 alone for half an hour and went to the room to have tea and breakfast with Mom.

"Is Akash okay?" Mom asked.

"Yes, but he is throwing up," said Dad. He sat at the breakfast table. It was his turn now to have his eyes welling with tears. He wasn't saying a word.

Finally, Mom said, "Let it out."

Dad hugged her and cried loudly. He said to Mom, "Our Shukla family is going through a really tough time."

They were back soon, then a young woman came into my room and said, "Time for physical therapy."

My heart immediately sank. I knew I was in for a tough session. Thankfully, she was talking to my roommate. He had bowed legs and had gone through corrective surgery on only one leg. He was a big, burly guy, about six feet two inches, with curly black hair. I listened closely to see what the therapist had him do, knowing I was in for much of the same later on. She had him stand up and take a few steps. To do this, he needed the assistance of three physical therapists. I thought to myself, "Oh shit. What I'm in for is twice as bad as what this guy is going through."

Half an hour later, another therapist came to my room. She was a sweet woman in her twenties. She said, "My name is Colleen. The goal for today is to sit you on the edge of the bed with your feet dangling."

I looked at Mom's face. She looked worried.

The therapist got on my right side and lowered the bed rail. She said, "First I want to rotate you ninety degrees." I grabbed the chain hanging from the bedpost and pulled myself up. Then Mom and Dad helped me turn. I was making loud sighs of pain and discomfort. Next, I had to slide towards the edge. There was no way I could do that on my own. Mom and Dad were pushing my upper body, and Colleen was pulling my legs. Surprisingly, Colleen got me to the position she wanted without too much pain.

Once my feet were touching the floor, I had to sit upright. This was quite difficult. She then asked me to move my ankle up and down, and do some easy ankle exercises. I sat for three minutes. Then I went back to my sleeping position. As she was leaving, Dad told her how I planned to write a book on this experience. She raised her eyebrows, looked admiringly at me, and said, "Wow."

I told her, "If they make a movie, I'll make sure that Julia Roberts plays you." She smiled. Once she left, I took a sigh of relief. This wasn't half as bad as I thought it would be.

The rest of the morning was rather uneventful. At one thirty, the leg pain was on the rise. It was tough to concentrate on anything other than the pain, so Dad had put a *Friends* DVD in the laptop. Chandler wanted to break up with Janice and was pretending that he was moving to Yemen. Janice goes to see him off at the airport. She wants to know the address at which she can write letters to Chandler and confirms his address, "15 Yemen Road, Yemen." I was laughing hard. The humor in *Friends* had eased the pain of this surgery in ways that I never thought possible.

At three thirty, a nurse came and gave me two pain tablets. I said, "I'm not in too much pain; why take pain medication?" She said, "That will help you switch from the pump to the tablets."

Ten minutes later, I was feeling a little nauseous. As Dad held the vomit tray, I emptied the contents of my stomach. I filled the whole tray, and then looked helplessly at Dad. He was standing there with a second tray. All this for two to three inches, I thought to myself. Everything I had put in my stomach since that morning had come out. So did the pain medication that I had taken. Shahnaz, a very pretty nurse, told me that I couldn't take the next oral dose of pain medicine until eleven thirty p.m., and told me, "Use the pain pump in the meantime."

Of course, the pump made me nauseous. This was a vicious cycle. Suddenly, the mood in the room had become very gloomy. Dad sat quietly on the sofa, and was holding his head in his hands. As he later told me, he was feeling very guilty. He said, "If *I* had said no to this surgery, we would not have done this." Mom looked at Dad's face, and asked him to walk out with her. She took him to the waiting room, and told him not to worry, and that everything would be all right. Dad said, "I'm not worried, just sad. Akash can barely talk. What have we done here?"

All my relatives came to visit that evening. Dad and Auntie were leaving for their room. Mom went with them. They had a quick bite, then Mom came back to spend the night in the uncomfortable chair. My relatives left. "Dad looked very worried," I said, "but I am doing okay now."

At ten, Dad called and asked how I was doing. I said, "I am doing much better. Why don't you come here for a few minutes and see for yourself?" Dad took the elevator from the fifth floor from across the street to the ground level. From there, he walked to another hallway and took an elevator to the second floor. He then crossed the bridge and came to the hospital building. Near the main elevator was a security guard, a young fellow in his thirties with an authoritative face.

As Dad tried to push the elevator button, the security guard asked him, "Where are you going, *Sir*?" There was so much sarcasm in the word *sir* that Dad knew he was in trouble.

Dad said, "My son is in room 514. He's in extreme pain. He wants to see me. My wife called me and asked me to stop by for two minutes."

"Your wife doesn't write the rules for this hospital, S*ir*," said the security guard.

Dad looked at the guard with worried eyes. How come this idiot can't sense my sadness? he wondered. He then said, "I know my wife can't make rules, but my son wants to see me."

The security officer said, "You need authorization; *do you under-stand?*" The "do you understand" was unnecessary and only meant to establish his authority. The security guard took Dad downstairs to an-other security officer. Downstairs, Dad repeated his story to the other officer. That officer asked some other nurse to take Dad upstairs. On his way upstairs, Dad told the nurse my story. The nurse was very sympa-thetic. As they reached the fifth floor, Dad said, "The insurance isn't picking up a penny. We're spending $200,000 for this." Her mouth dropped to the floor. She brought Dad to my room. As she started walk-ing away, Dad turned to her and said, "I'll be done in a few minutes."

"Take as long as you want," she said in a kind voice.

Dad was happy to see me feeling better and left in ten minutes. I had taken two tablets of Vicodin, the narcotic painkiller, and was very sleepy.

Day 2: I did not get up until nine thirty the next morning. Half an hour later, a doctor came into the room to remove the dressing. I told my dad quickly to start taking a movie. Up until that time, my legs be-low my knee were completely wrapped with white dressing. The doctor's scissors were shearing the cloth. A metal structure was slowly becoming visible. I looked down and saw the rings for the first time. I was in shock. There were these three substantially large external rings fixated to my leg bones with pins, wires, and bolts.

At around twelve, two therapists came in. "Today's goal is to have you stand up for about one minute. Do you have any questions?"

I said, with a mischievous smirk, "I have one question. Are you out of your fucking mind?" Everyone in the room laughed. I was brac-ing myself. I held the two bars on the walker. I was in a hunched-over position. I slowly lifted myself into a straight position. I stood up for roughly one minute. Then, they both lifted me and positioned me back on my bed. Mom asked me, "Was it painful?"

I said, in my Chandler style, "It wasn't painful. It was *VERY* painful." Mom and Dad felt a little better that even under this severe pain, my sense of humor was intact.

I took a long nap, then at four thirty, Shahnaz came in and told me it was time for my first "pin care." I had heard the phrase several times but did not fully know what actually would be done. It helped that Shahnaz was a hot nurse.

First, she dipped a six-inch cotton swab in a mixture of saline solution and hydrogen peroxide. Then she went around the site of each wire, each screw, and each bolt where they entered my flesh. She would wipe the wound and remove the dry blood around the metal. It was like someone pinching you right at the point where the screws were already creating a lot of pain. What made it even more painful was knowing that while she was cleaning the first pin site, there were

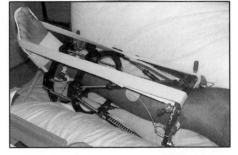

twenty-one more to go. Shahnaz was explaining to my mom every step. After Shahnaz did some, Mom started doing the rest. Mom is a focused individual with tremendous inner strength. She got the hang of it right away. The first pin care was finally over. I did not know at that time how this would become the most excruciating part of the daily torture.

In the evening, many relatives came to see me. Uncle Rajen commented that my face looked brighter and fresher than the previous day. I was indeed in a much better mood that evening. After the pain of pin care and starting physical therapy, as bad as it was, I knew that I could handle it. Though I was feeling better, at around seven thirty, I threw up again. The pill I had taken at seven had probably come out. At seven forty-five, I took another Vicodin. I slept most of the evening.

Day 3: The next day, Dr. Rozbruch came to see me. I hadn't seen Dr. Rozbruch since the surgery. He examined the pins and looked pleased. He said, "The pins look clean and the wounds are healing very nicely. I could release you today, except you need to be able to take a few steps first."

Dad asked him if he still thought we could do more than two inches. He said, "Two inches is no problem. To do more than that, Akash will have to exercise a lot."

After Dr. Roz-bruch left, they took me to fit footplates. Footplates were devices placed on and around each foot and then Velcroed to the rings. Its purpose was to keep my ankle at a ninety-degree angle. A nurse took me down-stairs, where they took 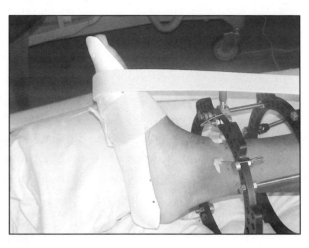 a piece of plastic and made it hot (and therefore malleable). Then by placing it on my foot, it was molded in the same shape.

At four p.m., a young man came in and said, "'I'm your PT. Let's see if you can get up." He had an assistant with him. He first moved my legs, and then he asked me to push my body towards the edge of the bed. Dad was standing behind me and pushing me. He could see how my hands were trembling. As I got ready to plant my foot on the floor, I started shivering. Mom quickly got a jacket and put it on me. My chin was chattering, my body was shivering, and the pain in my legs was unbearable. I thought my whole body was going to go into shock, and I was going to collapse. I gathered all my resolve and stood up.

However, in ten seconds, I could not bear the pain, and had to sit down on the edge of the bed. Everyone could see the agony on my face. I let out a loud sigh. The PT said, "I want you to try standing up one more time."

For the first time in this ordeal, I was losing heart and wanted to give up. Dad sensed that and he asked me, "Do you want me to take a movie when you do this the second time? That way we can record your pain." The idea of capturing this much pain and despair on video tape seemed intriguing. I said, yes.

The second time, I placed my hands on the rails of the walker, and quickly jerked up. The PT said, "Let's stand for as long as you can." Once I reached thirty seconds, he said, "Let's see if we can do it for one minute." At fifty seconds, the pain was unbearable and my arms were tired of holding up my body weight. I knew I could not stay standing for one more second. I leaned backwards and collapsed into my bed. We all knew at that time that leaving for home tomorrow was impossible, and the day after tomorrow was questionable.

At six, another physical therapist came to see me. Peter was six feet tall, probably in his mid thirties. His authoritative face made him look more like a doctor than a therapist. He spoke with confidence. "Today's goal is to stand for ninety seconds. You will first dangle your feet, you'll then put them on the floor, and then you'll slide towards the walker, place both hands on the walker, and stand for ninety seconds."

As I lightly put my feet on the floor, he separated them about nine inches apart and positioned them in a way that would make it easier for me to stand. The walker was a standard size. The rings on my legs were way too big. There was no way I could put both legs with rings inside the walker. We were slowly realizing that the hospital did not have all that much experience treating patients with fixators on *both* legs. I stood for ninety seconds, and that therapy session was over.

Immediately following my physical therapy session, a nurse came to give blood-thinning shots. Dad asked Mom to look at the pin sites. He was concerned that the surgery wounds might be flaring up. He stared blankly at the ceiling. He shook his head. He thought I was not listening. He said in a whispery yet angry voice, "This is a tough mother-fucking surgery. My God, this is not an easy surgery."

At nine, I asked Dad to take some notes for me. I started talking. "Even though I know my legs are straight, I feel like they are crossed. The pin sites are itching like a bitch, and I know I can't do anything about it. I wanted this extra height, so I have decided to take this pain with a sense of humor. When my future wife is going through child-birth, I will be able to tell her, 'Compared to what I have gone through, your pain is probably nothing.'"

Day 4: I woke up the next morning at nine thirty. My appetite was gone since the previous day's physical therapy. That physical therapy was a tough one.

When we came to New York for the surgery, we intentionally got my Jeep, thinking it would be an easier car. We had now changed our mind. We needed a lower car; otherwise, I would never be able to step up in the car. Mom went to New Jersey and brought back the Jaguar.

At eleven fifteen, Peter, the PT from the previous day, came in. He had gotten a wider walker. This would allow me to stand inside with both my legs. Since the surgery, I had not yet taken a single step. That morning, I was determined to walk a few steps. Peter got me to stand up, and then asked me to move my right foot forward while leaning on the left. Moving my foot six inches was like moving mountains. I was barely able to lift my leg.

Then Peter's assistant, El Meida, pushed my other leg forward. I have no words to describe the pain. Peter and El Meida showed great sensitivity and compassion. I said to them, "If you guys weren't as good as you are, this would be a much more difficult recovery."

The nurse behind me started laughing. She said, "This guy is good. He's going to be a politician." I walked two steps forward, and then slowly moved two steps backwards. The whole process took ten minutes. As I sat down, tired and exhausted on my bed, I had a triumphant smile on my face. The sense of accomplishment was stronger than the pain.

Dad said to Peter, "I own a manufacturing company and deal with complex issues every day. I used to tell Akash that he's not strong enough to deal with the complexities of a manufacturing company. I guess I have to take that back."

Peter and El Meida nodded smilingly. After they left, Mom asked me to eat something. I said "Hell, no."

Mom said, "How about just one banana?" I shook my head.

Dad then made a deal with me, "Eat a banana, and then we'll watch *Basic Instinct*." I had heard about that famous scene with Sharon Stone.

"Give me the damn banana and start the movie," I said.

At four, Mom started doing the pin care. She was handling this expertly. Dad, on the other hand, looked exhausted. I think watching me go through two painful therapies was too painful.

During the pin care, Richard, the nurse, was observing Mom. Richard was a pleasant looking nurse. He seemed well read. With his impressive mustache, you could easily take him for a character actor on Broadway. He was guiding Mom on the techniques. Dad was holding my hand with one hand, and covering his eyes with the other. Immediately after pin care was done, a nurse came and removed the IV.

Day 5: The next morning at eleven, Peter, the therapist, came with an assistant. They asked me to stand up. I wasn't looking forward to doing it. I was telling them jokes and chitchatting. "Less talk, more work," Peter said.

"You got it," I said, sitting down.

Peter said, "Whenever you're ready."

"I appreciate not being rushed," I said. I was still sitting on the edge of my bed. "Anytime now," I said.

I then mustered up all my energy and got up. I just could not put any weight on my feet and soon started to collapse. Peter quickly supported me. I was in a lot of pain. It felt like a thousand needles were piercing the place of the bone incision. Going home today was looking more and more doubtful.

Mom, by now, had caught a cold. The stresses and the lack of sleep for so many days had taken its toll. She was afraid I might catch her cold. She decided to sleep in the Bel-Air hotel room rather than in my room. That night, at midnight, my right leg had rotated on its side. My toes, instead of pointing to the ceiling, were parallel to the mattress. The pins were pushing up against the bone. I looked at my leg helplessly but could not rotate it back straight. With the leg bone cut in the middle, I had no strength to make my leg move.

I pressed the call button, and told the nurse to come help me. It took them some twenty minutes to come put my leg back in position. Staring at my leg in that gruesome position for twenty minutes, I kept asking myself, "What the hell have I done?"

One of the toughest things during the hospital stay was going "number one" and "number two." My dad would hold the plastic bottle for me. That is how I did number one. Number two was much more difficult. To get up from the bed and to sit on the commode would take me half an hour. Then when I was done, Dad had to help me clean up. One would lose all his dignity going through this. Dad tried to make me laugh about it. When I sat on the commode, he would sit next to me, hold my hand, talk about presidential politics, and call the whole event a "crap-conference."

We were hoping that September 29 would be the day when they would release me. It did not happen.

At six pm, Dad and I were having a very interesting conversation. Would Kerry do well in the upcoming election? Dad was sitting on a sofa in front of me. I said, "He's going to win."

"We will miss the debate tomorrow," said Dad.

I said, "That's too bad, I really wanted to see that debate."

Dad said, "But we will be doing something more important, like pin care or a 'crap conference.'" Yes, I was sitting on a commode, and Dad was keeping me busy with conversation so that I didn't concentrate on my pain.

Mom had not been looking good for the last two days. She was taking a lot of cough drops. Her eyes were swollen. Dad had what appeared to be a sty, and his eye was swollen. The stresses of the surgery were getting to Mom and Dad.

Day 6: On Thursday, September 30, the head nurse came and told me, "If the PT thinks you are ready, you can go home this evening." We were all frightened at the thought of spending another day at the hospital. Initially, I had expected to leave Monday, which looking back seemed comical. At ten thirty a.m., a doctor came in and started checking my movements. After a minute or two, he said, "I think you're ready to go home, but you need to get authorization from the Head Physical Therapist first."

At noon, a young man in a ponytail came into my room and told me that he was the physical therapist. I knew that my getting out of the hospital today would depend on my walking a few steps for him. The transfer from the bed to the wheelchair went smoothly. When I walked, it was painful. He wanted me to walk ten steps, but I could barely take five. I didn't think he would let me go that day. Mom and Dad looked worried. We all felt I was ready to go home, but we were also worried about the lack of my mobility. I sat down on the bed. I knew he wasn't going to discharge me today. He looked at me thoughtfully, looked at Mom, and then he said, "You are a bright family. I know you can continue this at home. I'm going to let you go today."

At two thirty, we left the room. Initially, only one nurse was going to help me get to the car. Thankfully, Shahnaz intervened and said, "This is a two-person job." As I later found out, it was probably a five-person job. As we were leaving the hospital, my heart was leaping with joy. Mom and Dad looked very happy. The nurses took me downstairs in a stretcher rather than in a wheelchair.

Once next to the car, it was very difficult for me to get into the car from a stretcher. Mom and Dad looked helpless. I could see their blood pressures going up. It was a simple task, getting in the car. But I could not put weight on my feet and could not move my feet. How do you get into the passenger seat and how do you slide your feet inside? It must have taken us fifteen minutes to get from the stretcher to the car. Soon we were on FDR Drive. We were going home.

The hour and a half ride seemed more like six hours. My Uncle Rajen and his wife, Neha Auntie, were going to meet us at home. So was Ziggy, from my dad's work. As we drove down my street, my heart started to beat quickly. I knew it would be a tough job to get out of the car. Dad pulled the car next to the garage. Everyone was waiting for me.

My first task was to rotate my body ninety degrees and get my legs outside of the car. That took about five minutes. Next, I had to stand up, turn ninety degrees, and sit in the wheelchair. I tried but I just could not. The shooting pain caused me to let out loud screams. Everyone watching looked stunned. I think they were thinking, "Why did we go through this?"

Then Ziggy came to the rescue. He stood in front of me, put his arms under my shoulders, and lifted me. He quickly turned and placed me in the wheelchair. I looked at the faces of Rajen Uncle, Neha Auntie, and Sushi Auntie. They had looks of blank disbelief on their faces. Uncle Rajen started pulling the chair back up the ramp, and Dad held my legs up by the rings and walked with me as Rajen Uncle was pulling my wheelchair backwards. As he was holding my rings, Dad said, "We are all treating you like a king." Everybody laughed. Suddenly the gloom was gone.

As they were pulling my wheelchair up the ramp, I started singing *"Pretty woman, won't you pardon me . . . ."* In the middle of the song, I asked Auntie, "Can you please get me a cold glass of water; I'm very thirsty." Then I continued singing, *"Pretty woman, I couldn't help but see, pretty woman."*

I guess I felt like singing because there was profound joy in my heart. Throughout the last four months, I had agonized over making this decision. I knew I wanted to do this, but deep down I was afraid I would chicken out at the last minute. So as they were pulling me on the ramp into my home, and I was looking at those black ugly rings bolted on my legs, I knew for sure that I had not chickened out. I had gone through with it.

I was going to be taller. Now there was no doubt about it.

13   First Few Days at Home

Once I got home on September 30, I did not have to go to see Dr. Rozbruch until October 4. That was when the distraction (lengthening) would begin. The first few days at home were mainly uneventful. The first pin care on October 1 wasn't very painful. I spent most of my first day in my bed. At first, I couldn't use the footrests on the wheelchair. The footrests were eighteen inches apart. There was no way I could put my legs with the rings on onto the footrest. We needed to push the footrest further out. Since I could not lift my legs by myself that meant someone had to hold my legs up by the rings and walk with the wheelchair. My dad sent a few people from his factory to pick up the wheelchair and make modifications. All the changes were made the next day. On the second day, I transferred from my bed to the wheelchair. I then wheeled myself to the refrigerator and got myself a glass of water. It felt great to be able to move around by myself after being restricted in the way I was for the last ten days.

Dad asked me to describe the pain. I said, "Where the pins enter the flesh, that's where I feel the pain. Sometimes, it's where the bone is cut." I said, "I know exactly where the bone is cut." It felt like, at the point of the cut, the two pieces were rubbing against each other.

I was taking Vicodin to control the pain, but for some reason, we thought we should take as few as possible. That, as we know now, was a mistake. On October 3, by ten in the morning my right knee was hurting a lot. Every single pin was hurting. When I sat down to eat, I found it difficult to sit upright. I was only able to sit leaning back. Therefore, Mom had to feed me. Mom and Dad didn't tell me at the time, but later when I watched the video, I could see the pain settling in on my face.

At nine that night, I stood up with the walker. I then put one foot forward, and then the second foot forward. Slowly, I walked ten steps. Oh my God! That was quite an accomplishment. Mom, Dad, and Auntie looked very happy. The next day we had to go see Dr. Rozbruch. We had not forgotten how tough it was to get me in and out of the car. Mom was on the phone the whole day. She was looking for an ambulance service experienced in transporting a patient like me. She found it. It would cost $600 for a round trip to New York.

The next day, the ambulance driver expertly moved my wheelchair from our kitchen, down the ramp, into the garage, and onto the elevator platform at the back of his ambulance. Once I was in the ambulance, the driver started fastening my wheelchair to two rods that were attached to the floor. Dad was sitting right next to me. We did not realize how uncomfortable it was to sit on a wheelchair in a moving car. My feet were touching the floor, and with every bump, I felt a surge of pain from my sole into the bone that was cut in half, and from there, to every pin that was sticking in my body.

As the ambulance was driving on Route 78, Dad told me that he read in the paper that today was the last day to register to vote for the general election in November. I had filled out the registration form and sent it to the township, but had not received any confirmation. I remembered in 1992, when Bill Clinton was running, my dad took me inside the polling booth. After Dad made his selection for the young governor from Arkansas, he asked me to pull the lever. That night, we were watching the election results, and when we saw that Bill Clinton won the election, I still remember my six-year-old heart was thumping with joy. Ever since that day, I had been looking forward to casting my own vote in a presidential election. So when Dad told me that today was the last day to register, I wanted to make sure that my application had reached the township.

The next half an hour, I wasn't thinking about my pain. I was on the phone with the Somerset county voter registration office, talking to one person after another. Finally, someone said, "Yep, you're registered." I hung up, breathed a sigh of relief, and then my pain was back for the rest of the trip to the hospital.

Once we got to 72nd Street, the driver quickly got me down. He then tilted the wheelchair backwards to get onto the curb. We were learning all these tricks on maneuvering the wheelchair. First, we went to the radiologist to get my x-rays done. It took two people to help me get on the table. Once at Dr. Rozbruch's office, we were greeted by their entire staff. After only a few minutes of waiting, one of the receptionists called me into the back room. Soon the entire team of doctors came in and started to look at my x-rays. We realized at that time that this type of limb lengthening on both legs must not be all too common. Dr. Rozbruch said that everything looked fine. He then said, "Arkady is going to get you the lengthening chart."

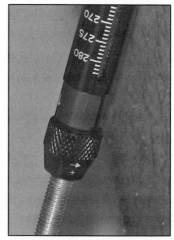

Dr. Arkady Blyakher came back several minutes later with the lengthening chart. He then handed a loose strut and a wrench to my dad to demonstrate how the lengthening was to be done. He showed my dad how each nut has to be rotated one complete turn in the direction of the arrow. When you rotated the nut 360 degrees, you felt a click. When you rotated one complete turn on all six struts, you moved the two rings, and therefore the bone at the point of the fracture, by one millimeter. Dr. Blyakher and my dad did the first set of extensions. Then we left the doctor's office. The next appointment was in fifteen days. I should be fifteen millimeters (a half an inch) taller by that day.

The ride back home was no better than the ride to the doctor's office.

From the next day on, we adjusted two struts in the morning, two in the afternoon, and two in the evening. Dad and I had created a routine for doing the adjustments. Dad would hand me the chart as he sat on the floor. Then he'd first look at the strut, and read the setting that it was on. I told him if he was correct, and then I told him what number it was supposed to go on. He would turn the nut one complete turn and tell me, "Okay." At this time, I would circle the number, indicating that it was complete. On each strut, every few days, we got a free day-that is, the strut did not need adjustment that day.

The top ring just below the knee was secured to the bone with wires and bolts. One wire was connected to either side of the ring, and went through the bone. Another wire, at a forty-five-degree angle from the first wire, also went through the bone. Then there were two slightly bigger bolts that went through the bone, but not out the other side. The bottom ring above the ankle was almost identical to the top, except it had bigger bolts. The middle ring was not connected to my leg through any pins or wires. However, the middle ring  was connected through the top ring through six adjustable struts, and it was connected to the bottom ring by four nuts and bolts.

Mom started doing pin care but needed more supplies. We needed six inch Q-tips, hydrogen peroxide, and Xeroform in 3/8 inch width. Dad went to purchase pin care supplies. To our great surprise, not a single surgical store in New Jersey carried a 3/8 inch-width Xeroform. The hospital had done a poor job of preparing us for pin care. In fact, my suggestion to doctors and hospitals would be to prepare Power-

Point training modules on pin care as well as on physical therapy. A patient and his family should be asked to attend a training program prior to the surgery.

Dad came back from the surgical supply store, frustrated. "They should have told us where to buy this from," he said. He got on the internet and found a website, Allegro Medical. It had everything we needed, only much cheaper.

Mom was working with me on bending my leg at the knee and exercising my ankle. By October 7, two weeks after the surgery, I could lift my leg by myself.

During this time, the pain was still manageable. I had to take pain killer medication about six to seven times a day; Aspirin, once a day; antibiotics, three times a day; and adjustments of the struts, three times a day. With this many things to do, it was difficult to keep track of what was done when. We quickly put a white erase board in the

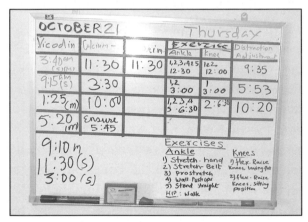

room, and made a chart for the activities during the day. Every time an activity took place, we wrote down the time. This made it easier to keep track of what was done at what time. The chart had six columns. In the first week of October, I had no idea that the number of columns in the chart was going to increase in a matter of a few weeks.

We had already done three days of distraction. The gap at the point of fracture in my tibia must have reached three millimeters. Yes, I was three millimeters taller. The pain was on the increase. Almost all day, I was in pain. Mom was religiously working with me to make me exercise. Mom made several calls to find a physical therapist. The hospital and the doctor had told us that we could do this ourselves, but Mom,

Dad, and I said, "Why take a chance?" Mom was trying to get a physical therapist to come to our home. No one agreed to that.

She then made an appointment with a therapist some seven minutes away from our home. Susan was a no-nonsense therapist. The first session went well. The therapy lasted thirty minutes. Mom wanted to make a second appointment in two days. Susan said, "I don't think you need that many sessions."

The next two days, the pain was steadily getting worse. At one point, as I was trying to get from the bed onto the wheelchair, a loud scream came out of me unexpectedly. Obviously, the distraction had changed things. That evening, as I was standing with a walker, I said, "I need to sit back down on the bed NOW." This had not happened until today. Mom and Dad looked worried. Dad quickly gave me one pain medication. Mom decided to give me dinner in bed. They quickly ate and then came back to my room for my exercises.

Mom was worried and made a second physical therapy appointment with Susan. Susan tried to talk us out of it but we thought that during the early stages of the lengthening, we did not want anything to go wrong.

The next day, Mom and I started to get ready to go to the therapy place at twelve forty-five. It took ten minutes to get in the car. It was a seven-minute drive to Susan's office in Green Brook. Dad met us there and helped Mom in getting me out of the car to wheel me into Susan's office. By the time we got in, it was one thirty. It took us forty-five minutes to get from my room to the inside of her office.

Then her therapy began. First, she gave me an ankle flexor (ProSt-retch), asked me to put my foot on it, and rock in and out to exercise my ankle joint. I did thirty on each leg. Then, using my walker, I stood up and walked six steps. Susan said that more than anything else, walking would help me the most because it forced me to put my body weight on

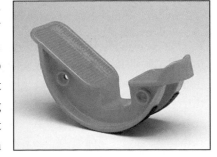

my ankle. Mom had reminded me to schedule my pain medication such that I took Vicodin just one hour before the appointment with Susan.

Susan worked with me for about half an hour. Fifty dollars per session seemed like a good bargain. On our way out, Dad ordered takeout: spaghetti with olive oil and garlic, and some broccoli. When we got home, it was a tough task to get me in the house. After that was accomplished, Mom went to pick up the food. I felt like I was eating much better than ever before in my life.

The next day, I started feeling unusual pain on my right leg. All the pins started hurting. As we moved the nuts on the struts, the strut assembly would elongate and push the rings apart. The rings were nailed and bolted to my bones, so all the pressure would be transmitted to the bolts, which would create a constant pain at the point where they entered my flesh and then bone. Foolishly, I did not take pain medication when I went to bed. Dad thought that if I could, I should get used to taking less pain medication. My dad is otherwise a phenomenal strategist. This one time- boy, was he wrong!

The next morning, I woke up at five thirty with unbelievable pain in my thighs. By this time, Mom and Dad had moved a second bed in my room. They had both started sleeping in my room. Mom gave me Vicodin right away. We went back to sleep. By the time I woke up at nine fifteen, the effect of the medication had worn off. I felt pulsating pain in my thighs. By the afternoon, I had a pounding headache. Mom started giving me a head massage. Dad jumped in the car, went to Drug Fair and Wal-Mart, and purchased three different types of massagers. We had surmised that the stretching was tightening all the muscles and that a gentle massage might alleviate some pain.

On October 10, the right leg wasn't hurting as much as the left leg. I was still doing all my exercises. By the afternoon, the thumping headache was back. I had glassy eyes and a painful face. At nine thirty, for the first time since the surgery, I broke down into loud sobs. Mom hugged me. I kept saying, "I can't take this pain; what do I do?"

Dad let me cry for a minute or two. Then he said, "This seems like the worst pain so far. Would you like to describe it on camera for our video library?" Silly as it may sound now, it seemed like a good idea then. Dad turned the camera on. I described my pain. Dad's trick was working. I became a reporter instead of a victim.

Many years ago, we had made a complete set of all the episodes of *LA Law*. We used to joke that one of these days, we would have time to watch some 200 hours of *LA Law* episodes. Well, that time had come. That night, we watched four one-hour episodes of *LA Law*.

Up until October 10, when Dad moved the nut one complete rotation, he used very light finger pressure. The cutting of the bone must have created some slack in that whole structure anyway, and the initial motion of the nuts must not have put that much force on my pins. By October 11, things were changing. The nut on the strut would move only after applying a lot of force.

I was receiving a steady stream of phone calls from my relatives all over the world. My doctor-cousin, Neha, made a quick trip from England to come visit me and cheer me up. Because of her medical background, she was able to do pin care expertly. She did it in half the time as Mom, but, as I jokingly complained, hurt me twice as much! Throughout her stay, she encouraged me to start doing many tasks on my own. Her sister, Paroo, was coming to see me next month. Many other relatives from outside USA were planning to visit me. These visits did help me forget the pain temporarily.

The pain, however, was on the rise. It had traveled upwards to my waist. My thighs were still hurting. On October 13, the pain was so unbearable that I again broke down into sobs. Mom massaged my thighs all day. Vicodin was not helping. In the afternoon, I was again in tears, but I also was determined that I wasn't going to give up. Mom was massaging my thighs, and Dad was holding my hand. At that time, I remembered the Indian movie I had seen, *Kabhi Khushi Kabhie Gham* ("The Cycle of Happiness and Sadness"). The hero, whose name in the movie happened to be Rahul, gives advice to his brother, who later ends up giving the same advice to Rahul's son. He said, "To become somebody, to achieve something important in life, you have to give it everything you have and listen to your heart. If your heart doesn't give you an answer, if it seems hopeless and you seem to be losing your resolve, then you close your eyes, and say the name of your mother and father. Then you will overcome all your difficulties and you will be victorious."

This was a very emotional scene in the movie. On October 13, as tears were rolling down my cheeks, I remembered that scene. I asked Mom and Dad to get closer. I hugged them, told them that dialogue from the movie and then said their names out loud. All of us started sobbing, but we all derived strength from that emotional experience.

October 15 was an important day. We had an appointment with Dr. Ilizarov. This was the first appointment after the distraction had begun. This time, we did not get an ambulance. We were using Mom's Jaguar for my trips to the therapists' offices and were doing okay. We left at eleven thirty a.m. for a two thirty appointment. There was very light traffic. We crossed the Holland Tunnel by 12:10 p.m. and were driving on FDR Expressway. Then Mom's cell phone rang. Mom was driving, and Dad was sitting next to me in the back seat. He picked up the phone. It was Dr. Rozbruch's office. "How come you're not here?" the receptionist asked.

"What do you mean?" said Dad, "We'll be there in an hour."

"But your appointment was at ten thirty a.m."

"You're kidding," said Dad. Then he said, "Hold on." He turned to Mom and said, "Our appointment was at ten thirty. Did you know that?" Mom had entered all of this into Microsoft Outlook Scheduler, but in the hustle of preparing for my trip, she did not check the calendar in Outlook and thought that the appointment was at two thirty. Dad said to the receptionist, "We will be there in an hour; is that too late?"

"It might be. But do your best. Get here as quickly as possible."

"How could this happen!" Dad was lamenting.

I too was very nervous. On that day, we were going to find out if the distraction was going okay. I said to Mom, "What's the point of going? Let's turn around and go home."

Mom kept saying, "Don't worry- they *will* see us."

We first had to go to the radiology laboratory two buildings away from Dr. Rozbruch's office. The wait for the x-ray could be anywhere from ten minutes to an hour. There was tremendous panic in us as we were approaching 72nd Street. Fortunately, we got the x-rays in twenty minutes. By one thirty, we were on our way to Dr. Rozbruch's office. They looked at the x-rays and said that the gap already measured ten millimeters, almost half an inch. This meant that I had reached the five feet mark. That was a great feeling.

The trip back to New Jersey was uneventful. That night, the pain from the pins was getting unbearable. I thought if I sat instead of slept, the pressure on the pins would be less. I tried sitting in a wheelchair, in a lounge, on the bed. Nothing helped. We then tried a different approach. Dad started a movie called *The Girl Next Door*. The movie starred a beautiful girl, Eliza Cuthbert. She was in the neighbor's backyard with her friend. She said, "Let's go for a swim." She then took off her top and her skirt. Wow, she had big boobs and a curvaceous, luscious body.

Suddenly, the pins were hurting a little less.

14   Pain Is on the Rise

As soon as I woke up on October 16, Mom got me started on various exercises. She said, "If we do this often, the joints will remain flexible and hurt less." She was right. The pain in my ankle and knee was at its maximum when I first woke up. Here is a list of the exercises I did every day:

Walk 10 Steps: For this exercise, I would transfer into the wheelchair. Mom would bring me to the kitchen and place the wheelchair about ten steps from the wall. I would get up from the chair and stand, using a walker. Then, putting all my weight on my two feet, I would lift the walker and move it forward about a foot. Then came the big task of moving the first leg one foot forward and then the second leg. This exercise wasn't always as easy as it may sound. The knees were hurting, the hip joints were hurting, and the incision point was hurting.

Wall Push-ups: Now that the prior exercise had brought me to the wall, I was ready for the next exercise. I stood about two feet from the wall. I then lifted my arms from the walker and placed them flat on the wall. Then, keeping my feet in place, I slowly moved my upper body towards the wall, in a push-up position, until my head was touching the wall. I would then push back to my original position. I would repeat this ten times. Mom or Dad always stood next to me in a position ready to catch me if I started falling.

Belt Stretch: This exercise required me to take a belt, put it around my toes, and then pull my forefoot towards me while keeping my knee straight. The challenge was to keep the belt in place. It kept sliding off. Mom tried various belt materials. Dad (the engineer) found a way

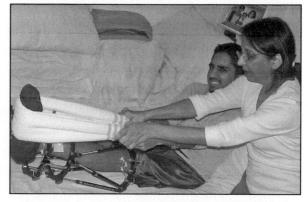

to fix this problem. He took his old Hush Puppy slippers and glued the belt at the bottom. I would put the Hush Puppies on and then pull the belt.

ProStretch: Once we saw this at Susan's office, Dad quickly searched on the web and purchased this for $40. I would stand up and lift one of my feet about five inches. Mom would place the ProStretch under my foot. I would place the foot on the top, and then rock it on the arc of the circle. I would do ten repetitions. Then she'd take it out from one side and move it to the other.

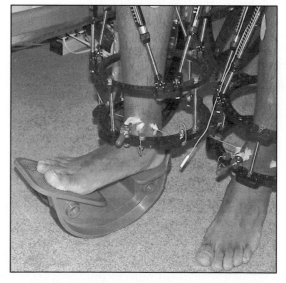

Knee Straightening: In this exercise, while sitting in my wheelchair, I would raise my leg straight at the knee and make ninety degrees with my body. I would do this ten times on each side.

Just Stand-Up: Placing the walker next to bed, I would put my arms on the walker, have my feet touch the floor, and then, with a jerky motion, stand up. Once on my feet, I would stand for three minutes. I did this routine five times a day.

By now, it had been three weeks since the surgery. The constant excruciating pain was taking its toll on me. There were times when the pain wasn't that bad, but there were times when every inch of my lower body was in constant pain. On October 19, I was in so much pain that it seemed meaningless to complain about it. I sat quietly in my bed. Mom came and sat next to me. She started massaging my thighs. I looked at her and said, "Thanks, Mom, but it is okay." Then I stared at the ceiling and said, "What is the point?"

Then Dad came to do the daily distraction. "Are you ready?" he asked me in a singing tone.

"Yeah, whatever," I said.

"What is the matter?" he asked.

I said, "What is the point, Dad?"

Mom and Dad knew my resolve was getting weaker. Later, Dad went upstairs and reviewed the database of all our digital pictures. He printed pictures of our relatives who were not very tall, but taller than me. He brought those pictures down. He said, "You have never thought of these relatives as very short. Guess what? After the surgery, you will be taller than them."

"No shit!" I grabbed the pictures from his hand. I kept staring at those pictures for a long time. There was a group picture where I was the shortest person in the group. Once the surgery was over, I would be taller than several people in that picture. I had said all day, "What is the point?" Now I knew the answer. My resolve was back.

That evening, a lot of my relatives came to see me. Once they left, we sat down to watch *LA Law*. A pin from my left leg was hurting more and more. By ten thirty, the pin gave me burning and radiating pain. I said, "The burning pain today is worse than it has ever been. Could this be a sign that the pin has been infected?" That would be a nightmare.

Mom looked at the pin and said, "No, it is not infected." I kept insisting that the pin was infected. Dad took my temperature, which was normal. There was dark pessimism in the room. Dad asked Mom to make sure we had a ready supply of antibiotic. Yes, we had it; Mom always takes care of everything. Mom then quickly went to the kitchen, signed on the internet, and researched on the symptoms of pin infection. She came back in fifteen minutes. "Burning alone is not an indication of infection," she said.

"Should we start the antibiotic anyway?" Dad wondered.

Mom reminded him, "Once we start, we have to do a ten day course."

The next day we consulted Dr. Rozbruch by phone. He said, "To be on the safe side, why don't you start the antibiotics?"

On October 23, Mom's elder brother Jitu and his wife, Bharti, came to see me from Canada. They are the most loving and caring people you would ever meet. They were calling us all the time to find out how I was doing. They were extremely worried about this procedure right from the beginning. They took a few days off from their busy schedule to come see me. They had driven all night to get to New Jersey. Soon after they came, Uncle Jitu asked me where I had the worst pain. He then said, "I can give expert massages." It was not right to have an older uncle give a massage to a younger nephew but these were special circumstances. He untiringly gave me constant body massages. Prior to surgery, I had prepared myself for a lot of pain at the point of incision. I had not expected that my thighs and my waist would hurt so much.

The next morning, Uncle Jitu and Aunt Bharti suggested that we do a special prayer session in my room. Dad has never believed in any of these things, but on that day, he readily said yes. I sat in my bed. We placed the pictures of a special god on a table in the corner and did a *Satya Narayana* prayer procedure. In that procedure, you have to read several sections of a story. The story talks about how, if you keep your faith in God, he will perform miracles and come to your rescue. Everyone in the room was taking turns in reading a section from a small booklet. Jitu Uncle would ask to pause from reading, turn to me, and translate the story into English. Everyone was working hard to hold back their tears. Then at the end, Dad asked to pass the book to him and he read the last section.

The gloom of my pain had created a dark cloud in this Shukla household and we were urging for a divine intervention.

15   Doctor Orders a Slowdown

On the morning of October 25, we were preparing for our trip to New York. Jitu Uncle had gone back to Canada but Bharti Auntie had stayed back to help Mom and Dad. We left for New York at ten. It was our familiar route- first, Route 78, then the Turnpike, the Holland Tunnel, FDR Parkway, and then 72nd Street. Once in New York, we had developed a standard routine. Mom would stop the car at the entrance of the parking garage. Dad would get out quickly to get the wheelchair out of the trunk. He would position it at forty-five degrees with the passenger door of the car and lock the wheels. Mom would come out and start taking several small bags and start hanging them on the wheelchair while Dad helped me slide from the car seat on to the wheelchair. Then as Dad rolled me towards the radiologist's office, Mom would drive away to park the car.

That day too, we went to the radiologist's office and got the x-rays done. Then we went to the second-story office of Dr. Rozbruch and quickly to one of the examination rooms. Dr. Rozbruch came not too long after we had settled down, and started looking at the pins. He said, "They are the cleanest pins I've seen today."

Mom's face was beaming with pride. Dad quickly turned the video camera on, and said, "You are making Meena very happy and proud.

Can you please say the same thing again so that I can get it on the tape?" Dr. Rozbruch was enjoying the humor that my family was displaying, and he playfully went along.

We started telling him about the increase in pain I had been experiencing. I said, "Doc, my hips, lower back, and leg muscles are in constant pain."

Dr. Rozbruch asked me what strength Vicodin I was taking. He then said, "Let's use a stronger dose."

Dad said, "Sometimes the pain is so severe, the only thing that works in taking his mind off the pain is watching R-rated movies."

Dr. Rozbruch said in a playful tone, "And if that's not enough, then even there, we'll have to crank it up a notch to the next level." It was clear that our doctor-patient relationship was turning into a much more comfortable and a friendly relationship.

Next, Dr. Rozbruch started feeling my muscles. He looked at me with a concerned look on his face. He said, "Your muscles are a bit tight." He then tried to get my ankle to the neutral position, but felt tightness in my calves. He said, "I think it would be best to slow down the lengthening for a while." He suggested that instead of doing all six struts a day, we do three one day and three the next day. I was a bit disappointed, knowing that the whole process would take longer because of this.

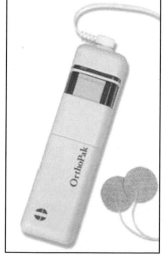

Then Dr. Rozbruch said, "Dr. Blyakher will give you a bone stimulator. He will show you how to wear it. It puts low voltage currents at the point of incision and accelerates healing. Make sure you wear it all the time." I did not know that this little device would become a constant nuisance for me for the next several months.

The stimulator was nothing more than a battery holder, and ran on a 9-volt battery. It came with a waist belt.

Two wires came out of the stimulator. At the end of each wire was a flexible stick-on electrode. You would stick the electrode on either side of the point of the cut at the bone. It would put 9-volt current and ultrasonic waves into your body. You would not feel it at all. If one of the sticky pads came unglued, as often it would, the damned thing would start an annoying beep. Such a treatment has proven to heal fractures faster. If this device sold at Radio Shack, it would probably sell for ten dollars. In a healthcare environment, it was $3,200- a tad more. Dr. Rozbruch knew we were paying for everything out-of-pocket and paying every bill ahead of time. He had also developed a special liking for my entire family. He said, "Don't worry about the cost of the device. We will cover it."

Soon Doctor Blyakher came in. We had met him many times before. He seemed to be in his fifties, bald, and had a lot of nervous energy around him. When he started to attach the electrodes on my leg, I asked him, in a worried voice, "Is this going to hurt me?"

He said, "No, you won't even feel it."

I quickly decided to have a little fun with him. He placed the sticky electrode on my leg right above the point of incision. As soon as he did that, I let a loud, painful scream out. He jumped and said, "What happened?" He looked puzzled. He then looked at my dad and said, "I have not even put in the batteries."

I started laughing. Dr. Blyakher knew he had been had. He started laughing too and said, "Don't be a wise guy; you scared me!"

Once home, Dad quickly prepared a new chart in Excel for the slower extraction rate. Over the next few days, Bharti Auntie looked after me and helped me take my mind off the pain. During pin care, she played the card game *UNO* with me. We also watched several Indian movies. She would help me exercise. She altered my clothes and attached a zipper on the side of my shorts so that I could put them on and off easily. The next weekend, her daughter, Sejal, and her family came to see me from Boston. Sejal's kids call me Akash Uncle! I enjoyed hearing that. I had a lot of fun with them. At times, I would forget about my constant pain. Bharti Auntie and Sejal's family left that weekend.

The pain seemed more sometimes and less some other times. The hip joints were hurting as if I had just run in a marathon. The thighs were constantly pulsating with pain. After my last visit with Dr. Rozbruch, I had started walking even more than I used to. This was a counterintuitive cure. When I was in more pain, I would have to walk more so my muscles would relax more and the pain would lessen.

By October 28, I was walking better. When we went to see our therapist, Susan, I was able to move comfortably from bed to wheelchair to her exercise bench. At the time, we thought Susan was doing a good job. We had no point of reference. Only later did we find how much more energy a physical therapist puts into fixing this kind of condition.

By October 29, my muscles did not feel as tight as they did a week ago. Dad wanted to increase the pace of distraction. He said, "This is a dilemma. If we do it slower, there is less pain but it will take longer to reach the desired height. The longer it takes, the more chance of infection there is. We have to find the right balance. Maybe we should reach a compromise, and do four struts a day instead of three." He then wrote a long letter to Dr. Rozbruch. I have included the letter below:

From: Shukla Meena & Rahul

Sent: Saturday, October 30, 2004 1:49 PM

To: 'Rozbruch, S. Robert MD'

Subject: Akash Update October 30, 2004

Hello Dr. Rozbruch,

Akash is doing very well. It has been a marked improvement from last week.

Pin Condition: Pins look the best they have so far. The one pin, which looked reddish last week, is back to normal. His burning pain from that pin is gone. All other pins look like they are healing nicely. The oozing is the least it has been since the surgery. We have stopped the antibiotics after a seven-day course.

Other Pain: The extreme pain Akash complained about in the hips and thighs is back to moderate pain. His headache is gone. Overall, it has been the best week we had since the distraction began. He has been sleeping well without the aid of sleeping pills. He does need to take one 10-mg. pain pill every four hours.

Swelling of Ankles: The slight swelling we had noticed last week is gone.

Distraction: As per our discussions in your office, effective last Monday, we have reduced the rate of distraction down to a half a millimeter per day. I prepared a new chart in Excel, where I adjust struts 1, 2 & 3 on each leg one day and 3, 4 & 5 on each leg the second day. The nuts move a little more freely than they used to last week. His muscles, which seemed all tensed out last week, seem a bit more relaxed. The only down side is, if we keep at this pace, the next one inch will take us into December 23, and if we can go the third inch, it will take us into the middle of February.

Exercise: Akash has picked up the pace of exercise and follows a vigorous schedule.(Those R-rated movies are quite a motivator!) I have attached a photograph of our daily activity board, which shows the various activities he does during the day. In my lay, non-medical opinion, his ankle and knee movements look excellent.

My Suggestion: The reduction in the pace of distraction seems to have helped big time. Of course, nothing in life is simple. By extending the overall period of distraction, we have to contend with the possibility of a slight increase of the risk of any future infection. I was wondering if we could increase the pace of distraction moderately. What if we increase the distraction from three struts a day to four struts a day? That would be only a 33 percent increase. That way, I can do struts 1, 2, 3, 4 on day one; 5, 6, 1 & 2 on day two; 3, 4, 5 & 6 on day three; and so on. It may seem like a difficult sequence to follow and could go out of sync, but I am confident I can prepare a new chart and follow it correctly. If you would like, I can send you a sample chart for you to look over.

We will continue the current pace of three struts a day, and I will wait for your instructions. If you agree, I would like quickly to go to four struts a day. If the pain increases, we can always come back to the current pace. Please let me know what you think.

-Rahul

The above message was sent at 1:50 p.m. By 7:50, Dr. Rozbruch sent us the following response:

Things sound good. You can make the transition to four struts per day and see how it goes.

Thanks for the update. Did he try a muscle relaxant called Baclofen? If not, that can also be helpful. Let me know.

S. Robert Rozbruch, MD

We were all very happy that I started doing .67 millimeters a day but the pain was getting worse again. The next few days were uneventful, except for the general election. On November 2, I was scheduled for physical therapy at Susan's place. Mom got me in the car at two thirty, and drove me there. Dad met us in the parking lot, and helped me get into the office. Once we were in the therapy room, he said, "I have some good news."

"What?" I thought this must have something to do with my surgery.

He said, "Kerry is ahead."

"How do you know?" I asked him.

"I was looking at some special websites, which somehow have access to some exit polls, and they all say Kerry is ahead," Dad replied.

This was very good news. It would certainly make the pain of surgery go away for many days. After therapy, Dad, Mom, and I were driving to the polling booth, where I was going to increase Kerry's victory margin by one vote. As we got in the car and drove to the polling booth, all three of us were flying high.

"I knew there would be justice in the end," Dad said, getting all emotional. I was extremely happy. I had followed this election closely, watching all the debates. After the first debate, we were thrilled that Kerry had done a masterful job. We couldn't believe our good luck. We had wanted a change for a long time. I was imitating George Bush and his recurring line in that debate, "We've been working *hard* . . . ." Then of course, that Saturday on *Saturday Night Live*, Will Forte did a hilarious portrayal of George W. Bush.

On November 2, on our way to the polling booth, I was repeating all of those lines to Dad. I was on cloud nine.

That evening, we finished our dinner early. We were in a celebratory mood. We quickly positioned ourselves in front of the TV. We were determined to enjoy every single moment of our sweet victory. We kept a bottle of champagne handy and would open it when Kerry reached that magic mark of 272 electoral votes. That is what we had done in 1992 when Bill Clinton won the election.

It was a sad and heartbreaking night. The early exit polls turned out to be wrong. Kerry lost the election. My pin pain was back in full force.

16 The Dark Days Are Coming

The next morning I woke up with a very bad headache. Some of the muscle pain was also back. At times, the pain would be so severe that I would talk funny. While in mid-sentence, I would get strange pain signals, which would cause me to jerk up my neck and repeat the last word I had just said. Mom and Dad laughed at it first but then started getting concerned. Dad said I behaved as if I had Turret's Syndrome. Frequently my chin started chattering. The upbeat mood of the previous week was gone. The right pin on my right leg, which was burning the previous week, had started burning ten times more.

As if I did not have enough problems, I had to deal with one more new problem. For all these days, every night, I had to wear footplates to keep my ankle in the neutral position. On November 4th, I got up early. The sole of my right foot was hurting a lot. Wearing the footplates all night had created a tender spot on my forefoot. There was a distinct dark red circle, about one inch in diameter, on my sole, and it was burning like a bitch. I did not need this additional complication in my life. On November 6, the bottom of my foot was hurting so badly, there was no way I could put the plates on my foot. I still put them on before going to sleep but then woke up at two a.m. screaming with burning pain. Mom had to take the plates off.

The pain near my ankle on my right foot was becoming unbearable. Dad said we needed to create a somewhat objective way to get a handle on the pain level. He created a chart where every four hours, I would rate the pain on a scale of one to ten. I would rate it for my knee, ankle, hips, thighs, and at the point of incisions. On November 6, I rated my pain at eight.

By November 7, the burning pain at the pins was getting worse. I rated my pain at ten for each body part. We talked about increasing the dosage of pain medication and taking it every four hours on the dot. How else could we fight the onset of this pain?

I did not know it yet, but a combination of three things was setting the stage for a major crisis. One, because of the extreme pain, it was a little more difficult to follow my exercise plan. Two, we had decided to increase the dosage of pain medication to every four hours. And three, the footplates could not be put in place at night. We still thought that everything was moving ahead quite well. There was excitement in the entire family that this surgery was heading towards a great success. We knew that reaching two inches would be a piece of cake, and that with all the efforts my family and I were putting in, three inches was possible. Hell- three and a half inches was not out of the question. We did not think for a minute that we would have to stop lengthening before reaching my goal. I still had a hopeful outlook on things.

I had no idea what was in store for me.

17 New Complication: Throwing Up

November 10 started like a normal day. Dad left for work. He was invited to speak at a career fair at my school. I had worked with Dad on his PowerPoint presentation. It was funny and inspirational. I could not wait to hear how it was received.

I got ready, had a hardboiled egg, cereal, and a chocolate chip waffle for breakfast. After breakfast, I went to lie down in my room. The pain had suddenly increased. I tried to watch TV for a while. I then thought of checking the website of Drexel University. I was thrilled to have been accepted at Drexel and was itching to start my study of mechanical engineering in September of 2005.

As I was sitting in front of the computer in the kitchen, I started feeling a little funny in my stomach. Five more minutes and the funny feeling was back. I thought I would throw up soon. I raced my wheelchair to the bathroom. My mom thought I was on my way to use the bathroom. Then she heard the retching and gagging sounds coming from the bathroom. She came running. I threw up for a good five minutes. Everything I had eaten since morning came out. Sushi Auntie quickly got me a glass of water. Mom helped me back in my bed. I had a sick lingering taste in my mouth. I wanted to go back to check the website at Drexel. Mom and Auntie said I should go to bed and take a rest for a while.

Later I checked the daily picture of the white board for the previous day to see how much medication I had taken. I had taken Vicodin at eight thirty, twelve thirty, five, and eleven. I took my daily calcium tablets at ten a.m., five p.m., and seven forty-five p.m. I took a muscle relaxant at ten a.m., six p.m., and ten p.m., and I took Aspirin at five p.m. and ten thirty p.m.

Back to November 10: I stayed in my bed for half an hour. Then I was up and about, back into my wheelchair. I had forgotten about that isolated episode in the morning where I threw up like crazy. Dad called on his way to my school. "How is Akash doing?" he asked.

Mom said, "He is doing fine. He threw up earlier but he is completely okay now. Don't worry about a thing."

Few minutes later, I was in the kitchen and then I said, "*Oh God*, I am going to throw up again." I rushed to the bathroom. Seconds later, Mom and Auntie were standing next to me. They were helplessly looking at me as I was emptying my stomach. I was tired and exhausted. I knew Dad must have finished his speech. I called him and told him about my second vomit. He sounded very worried. I said, "Dad, I don't need this shit right now."

On November 11, we had a scheduled visit to Dr. Rozbruch's office. Rozbruch was out that day. We had an appointment with Dr. Ilizarov. She said, "The pins look good. There is no infection." The x-rays looked good, too. All was well.

We asked her, "What is the maximum height increase that has been accomplished for stature lengthening?" She gave us a roundabout answer that meant nothing. Dad asked about my joint and ankle motion. Was it better than average, worse than average, or average? She gave another roundabout answer. On the way home, we were talking about how only Dr. Rozbruch gives confident answers.

November 12 was an uneasy day from the beginning. I was in severe pain. I was taking out my irritation on Mom and Auntie. I was complaining about my pain, my bed, food, everything. Then I told Mom, "I can't take this for a minute longer." I told her, "I want to scream."

Mom did not say anything; her eyes were filled with tears. She turned to Sushi Auntie and said, "I don't know what I can do to make him comfortable." She started sobbing. She then called Dad and told him, "Akash is not feeling well." Dad came home soon. He calmed me down. He said we should watch *LA Law* after lunch.

I was not hungry at all. Mom and Dad reminded me that my body needed nutrients to build new bone at the point of incision. I said, "You eat. I will take a nap." I went to my bed.

Dad said, "Let me sit next to you." He got on my bed and sat next to me.

In a minute or so, I said, "I think I am going to throw up." He quickly reached for the vomit tray. He positioned it for me. I started throwing up. A lot of stuff came out with so much force, as if my stomach was saying, "I'm not going to keep anything you send to me. I'm sending it back."

Next day was the Indian holiday, Diwali. It is somewhat equivalent to Christmas. All my relatives came to our house for Diwali dinner. I was okay, or so I thought.

But then I threw up.

What we thought was a 24-hour virus was turning into something much worse. Dad quickly sent an e-mail to Dr. Rozbruch that night. Dr. Rozbruch called me in the morning. He said he had already called my pharmacy and prescribed a different painkiller, Darvoset, instead of Vicodin. He said he also had prescribed something for nausea. We were all relieved. Obviously, it *was* the Vicodin that was doing this. The new medication would make things better.

On November 15, Dad's friends Prakash Uncle and Rajul Auntie came to see me. Rajul Auntie brought a beautiful blanket that she had knitted for me. I was in much pain and sat quietly. We then played *PIT*, a fast-paced commodity trading game. That changed the tempo and we started laughing. After Prakash Uncle and Rajul Auntie left, Dad went to pick up Auntie, and Mom started doing pin care. By the time Dad came back, I was feeling nauseous again. Dad said, "Maybe you just have an upset stomach and should try going to the toilet."

I said, "Why not?" Once I went to the toilet, my stomach did feel better. That's it, just some gas, I thought. Five minutes later, I threw up.

The next morning I got up with extreme pain and my right ankle looked swollen. This surgery was turning out to be tougher by the day, and we still had twenty-five days left for the distraction. Twenty-five days seemed like a lifetime. How would I survive emotionally for that much longer? I wondered.

Dr. Rozbruch had suggested that we should consult with Dr. Wagner, an expert on pain management. Mom quickly made an appointment to see Dr. Wagner for November 18. Since we were not sure if it was the pain medication or some other virus, Mom called our doctor friend Dr. Bharti Shah. Dr. Shah was my pediatrician from my birth until July when I turned 18.

When Mom called her, Dr. Shah said, "Come see me right away." Dr. Shah was not in favor of such a surgery and in her own gentle way, had suggested that we not do it. But when I saw her in her office, she said, "You know I was not for this procedure but now that you have gone ahead with it, let us do everything to make it a great success." What a kind and loving attitude! She asked me to go for a blood test and stool test. Mom took me directly from her office to a lab.

The next morning, we drove to New York to see Dr. Wagner. On our way, Mom was constantly on the phone, talking with the lab people and trying to see if they could send the blood test results to Dr. Wagner's office. They said no, but Mom wasn't giving up.

Dr. Wagner was a pleasant and an engaging man. He seemed genuinely interested in helping me. Unlike some other doctors, once he was in the examination room with us, he seemed in no hurry to get out. While in Dr. Wagner's office, Mom called the lab again and got them to fax the test results to Dr. Wagner. Dr. Wagner looked at the results and said, "The white blood cell count is slightly elevated. This suggests a possibility of infection." The normal range is between 4 and 10.5. My count came in at 17.9. Dr. Wagner called Dr. Rozbruch. They discussed the white blood cell count for a while and then concluded that it was not high enough to justify a diagnosis of infection. Dr. Wagner said, "Let's stop Darvoset and try something else." He switched me to Hydromorphine, 2 mg, and told me to take it every four hours as needed.

We got back home in the evening. Dad went and picked up the new prescription. There was new hope in our hearts. This project was going to be back on track, we thought. I threw up the next day. The change in medication was not yet working. What was more, my left knee was completely frozen. I could barely bend my leg. My motion was never this restricted since the distraction had started. Dad decided that we should stop distraction for a day or two. He did not even call Dr. Rozbruch. He knew that we could not afford to lose any more motion.

On top of all this, two pins on my left leg looked swollen. The shooting pain from the thighs continued. It was way too much to handle. I was losing my will to keep going. The next day, Mom and Dad put me in the car, as difficult as it was to move me, and took me to a nearby guitar store. I didn't play guitar, but had always wanted to learn. Mom and Dad wanted to create some positive energy. At the store, there was no way they could take the wheelchair through the front entrance. The store manager opened his back door to let us in.

Once inside, I looked at various types of guitars. Then another salesman came and asked me why I was in a wheelchair. I asked him, "Do you really want to know?" I then lifted my pants and showed him the external fixators. He had a stunned expression on his face. I explained how the surgery worked. He looked at me admiringly. Then as he walked away, he said, "I'm proud of you, dude. That takes a lot of courage. I don't think there are many people that could do this. Good luck to you." The guy, I do not even know his name, would never know what his words meant to me. More than the guitar, his words gave me a new resolve. The trip to the guitar shop had already paid off.

During this time, we were desperately experimenting with various theories about the vomit problem. Dad theorized that the muscle relaxant I started a few weeks ago might have caused the problem. I stopped taking it on November 17. By November 20, I started taking Tums. Maybe it was acidity that was doing this, we thought. I did not throw up on November 21. We were delighted. The Tums therapy was working. That sense of good feeling was short lived. I threw up the next day.

That was a tough ten days for me. My ankle movement did not look good at all. With all the throwing up, I had very little energy to exercise. Still, on November 21, I did the ankle-hand stretch four times, ankle-belt stretch three times, three minutes standing four times, ten step walking three times, knee flex sitting three times, knee flex in bed five times, wall push-ups once, and ankle ProStretch twice.

We had an appointment to see Dr. Rozbruch on November 23. Little did we know that our world was going to crumble on that day.

18   "Stop Lengthening"

We were scheduled to see Dr. Rozbruch on November 22. That morning, I was up at three thirty with severe pain. Mom gave me a Hydromorphine at four and then I went back to sleep. By six, we were up again. Going to New York was always a tremendous chore. We had to pack all my medication, my wheelchair, walker, the vomit tray, and a few pillows in an attempt to keep me comfortable in the car. Then Dad always took his laptop with a DVD player and a few DVDs of *Friends* for me. The car ride was always uncomfortable and painful. Watching old episodes of *Friends* was a welcome diversion.

I had my breakfast at seven thirty. All seemed well. I was hoping the trip to New York would be uneventful. The worst of times I thought was behind us.

Then I threw up.

The mood turned gloomy in no time at all. We left for New York and were quiet in the car. We got there in record time, only one hour and twenty-five minutes. Maybe this was our lucky day after all, I thought.

As usual, we went to the radiologist where I was x-rayed, and then headed up to Dr. Rozbruch's office. There was nobody in the waiting room. That meant that we'd be in and out fairly quickly. Dr. Blyakher quickly came in, and told us that according to the x-rays, I had reached thirty-six millimeters of distraction.

I told him, "That is exactly what our distraction chart says we should be at."

Then Dr. Fragomen came in. He was Dr. Rozbruch's assistant and probably his right hand man. He was a young fellow, but without hair, looked a little older than his age.

Dr. Rozbruch came in not too long after. "How are you doing Akash?"

I told him that things could be better.

He said, "We should reach the two inch mark on December 18th. I was thinking about doing the second surgery on December 24. What do you think?"

I said, "I don't like that." My cousin Anisha, from England, was planning to come spend Christmas with us. She was making this trip especially to cheer me up. I was really looking forward to her visit. I didn't want to spend those four or five days drugged up in the hospital. I said, "My stomach isn't cooperating. I threw up before I came to see you. What's going on with me, Doctor?"

He said, "I don't think it is related to this surgery. You should go see a gastrointestinal expert."

Mom told Dr. Rozbruch she was sure one of the pins was infected.

"Which one?" he asked. Mom pointed to a pin. He looked at it, looked to my concerned mom, and said, "No, this looks fine." He then started checking my ankle flexion. His expression changed from jovial to concern. He said, "Akash, your muscles and nerves seem very tight. Have you been exercising?"

I told him, "Vigorously."

"Let us try one more time," he said, and pushed my ankle back to neutral position. I let out a soft, pained scream.

"What happened?" he asked.

I said, "When you did that stretch, the right three toes on my right foot started burning."

Dr. Rozbruch did not seem happy to hear that. He said, "Let's try it again." He moved my ankle the same way. I felt the same pain, and let out the same scream. He said, "Describe what is happening to you."

I said, "When you push the ankle all the way in, it feels like someone is holding a flame up to my right three toes."

He looked at Dr. Fragomen. Dr. Fragomen looked back at him as if they communicated with each other in a silent language. We knew that they were about to tell us something serious. Next, Dr. Rozbruch started tapping various points on my leg, asking me if there was any funny sensation where he tapped. I told him no.

Dr. Rozbruch took a deep breath and said, "The distraction of the bone is stretching your nerve." His tone had completely changed. There was no levity. He said, "Listen, we don't want any nerve damage. The nerve is either getting irritated or being pinched." He then turned to Dad and said, "At this point, we have three options. The first option is to stop the lengthening now," .

I was in state of disbelief. Why was he talking about stopping the distraction? Did he want to stop it for the time being or did he mean, stop permanently? Rozbruch turned to me and said, "You have already reached thirty-six millimeters. Maybe that is enough."

Shit, he *was* talking about stopping permanently.

"The second option is to go into surgery again, do a soft tissue release on the gastronomies muscle, and add a permanent footplate on both feet, with pins going through each foot." Mom, Dad, and I all shook our heads. We were not ready for additional pins in my legs.

"The third option," he said, in such a pessimistic way that we knew he did not consider it much of an option, "would be to wait for a few days, and then try starting to lengthen again- though more than two inches is now extremely unlikely."

We were in a state of shock. I couldn't believe what I was hearing. This project was coming to an end way too soon. After all that I had gone through, I couldn't imagine having to stop lengthening at a little more than half of our goal.

"Well, think about it; we have a few days to decide," said Dr. Rozbruch. Then he and Dr. Fragomen left the room. Dad was staring at the ceiling, Mom was staring at my fixator, and I was staring at them. We did not say a word for a few minutes.

Dad broke the silence. He said, "There is a way out of this. We're not going to give up. There's always a way out."

Mom said, "We need a much better physical therapist."

"We don't have much time." My parents were talking rapidly.

"Dad, I can't take pins in my ankles. I would go nuts," I said.

As Dad navigated the wheelchair out into the hallway, Mom stopped by the receptionist's desk. She asked, "Can you give me the names of the therapists that you've worked with before?" Omaira gave her the list of several therapists. Only one of them was in our area, Jersey Central Physical Therapy in Edison, New Jersey.

As we were driving out of the parking lot, Mom got on the phone and started calling one physical therapist after another. Looking back, I know that this was a pivotal moment. We were just handed rather grim news, but rather than feeling sorry, my parents were searching for a way out. They both seemed to think there was a way out. That gave me tremendous hope.

Mom first wanted to contact a therapist named Mary Anne who she knew through her swim club. She called her at work but Mary Anne did not answer. Mom then called her at home. Somebody answered the phone and said, "She's not here." Mom does not give up easily- or maybe at all. She said, "I am her friend from swim club. I need her help regarding my son's surgery. Is there any way I can get in touch with her?"

Mom got Mary Anne's cell phone number. Just having her number made us feel hopeful. Now all Mom had to do was convince her to give me therapy at home. Dad said to Mom, "Tell her she can charge how ever much she wants to."

It really made sense to find a therapist willing to make house calls. Any time we had to go to their office, it was very difficult to transport me. From my bed to the car was a half an hour journey. When we reached our destination, getting out of the car and into the therapist's office was another half an hour journey. It was painful for me, and tiring for the person who was taking me there. A lot of aggravation would be avoided if someone would come to our house. A new person might also be able to motivate me better. We were hoping that Mary Anne would say yes.

Mary Anne said no. Mom pleaded with her. "You can pick your time- middle of the day, end of the day. You can pick your day and price."

Mary Anne said, "I'm sorry; I just don't make house calls." Mom hung up, but had no time to be disappointed. She then called Jersey Central Physical Therapy, which is about a forty-minute drive from my house. Mom had called them a month ago and asked about house calls. They had said no. This time too, Mom once again tried to get somebody from Jersey Central to make a house call. The answer was once again a firm no. She turned to Dad and asked, "Should I make an appointment anyway?"

"Why not?" said Dad.

Mom explained to the receptionist that she needed an appointment right away. Another roadblock- there was nothing available until the following week. Mom calmly explained our situation to the receptionist. "I need something tomorrow," she said. My mom is a persistent woman. If you're considering this surgery, you need a mom like her.

"Two thirty p.m. tomorrow." She got what she wanted. Then she started asking a lot of questions. "How many therapists do you have? Who will work with Akash? Does that person have experience with limb lengthening?" She hung up and said to Dad and me, "They say they have worked with these kinds of patients before, but who knows?"

It was two thirty in the afternoon as we got off the Roosevelt Parkway and drove toward the Holland Tunnel. Mom was now working on the next problem, making an appointment with the GastroIntestinal (GI) expert. We were in luck, as Dad's primary doctor, Dr. Goyal, happened to be a GI expert. Mom called my primary doctor and our family friend, Dr. Shah, gave her a quick update, and asked if she could do us a favor and call Dr. Goyal. It was so sweet of Dr. Shah to call us back and tell us that we got an appointment for four that afternoon.

Getting into Holland Tunnel sometimes takes ten minutes, sometimes an hour. That day, it took us an hour and a half. By the time we got out of the damn tunnel, it was already four. Mom called Dr. Goyal's office. "Can we change the appointment from four to five thirty?" she wanted to know.

"Dr. Goyal leaves the office at five. You can go to his Perth Amboy office," said the receptionist.

"Maybe we can see him there," Mom said.

"Perth Amboy is a walk-in. We cannot give you an appointment," the receptionist said.

Mom said, "We'll take our chances. Just give us the address."

By this time, I had a splitting headache. We went home, and Dad rubbed oil on my scalp and gave me a massage. I took a short nap, knowing I still had a lot ahead of me that day. After waking up, we all went to see Dr. Goyal.

His office was in an inner-city-like area. People in the waiting room were probably wondering why I was sitting in a wheelchair. In order not to freak others out, I had covered my legs with a blanket. The waiting room was very crowded. There was hardly a place even to stand. Dad was afraid someone would bump into my frames. I was extremely tired from the trip to New York, and was in a lot of pain.

Then Dad whispered to me, "Take off the blanket so people can see the frames." Once I did that, I could feel a silent gasp in the room. Dad then told Mom to position me in a way that the receptionist could see me. Dad walked to the receptionist and said, "My son has gone through a very serious surgery." He pointed his fingers towards my legs. He didn't say anything for a second. He wanted the sight of the frames to settle into the nurse's mind. "Is it possible to put him into a more comfortable area?" Dad asked.

"Absolutely," said the receptionist. She then took us to a back room, which looked like a document storage room.

Soon Dr. Goyal stopped by briefly and said, "I just want you to know, I cannot see you out of turn." That meant we would be there for hours. Then, in ten minutes, he came and said, "Let's go to the other examination room." He *did* see us out of turn.

Dad gave a quick summary. "Akash was very courageous in going through the limb lengthening surgery, but he has been throwing up for ten days, can't do his exercises, and his ankle is losing movement. Unless we find a solution to the vomiting problem, the height extension will have to stop, which would be a shame, especially after what Akash has already gone through."

Dr. Goyal listened attentively and then started examining me. He pressed against several parts of my stomach, asking me if it hurt. I said no. He turned to Dad and said that he didn't think it was a stomach virus or an infection. "However," he said, "It could be gallstone- but I doubt it."

Dad said, "If it is, how long does it take to fix it?" His concern was whether it would take weeks or months to fix that. And if it was months, what would happen to the distraction? Dr. Goyal said, "I don't think it's gallstones so there's no point discussing the treatment now."

He prescribed a new anti-nausea medication and told me to take Colace, an over-the-counter stool softener. Dr. Goyal also ordered a sonogram so we could rule out the possibility of gallstone problems.

During the ride back home, we felt confused and helpless. The pain management doctor thought that my sickness wasn't pain medicine related, but GI related. The GI specialist thought it wasn't GI related but pain medicine related. I was starting to lose hope. Maybe thirty-six millimeters was going to be it, I thought.

By that time, I was feeling hungry, which was a good sign. Mom called Café Giardino, a neighborhood restaurant, and ordered spaghetti with marinara sauce on the side. We stopped by Drug Fair and picked up Colace, then the food. After we got home, I had some spaghetti, but after several bites, felt nauseous and stopped eating. Then Mom did pin care. It was midnight and I had yet to do my daily exercises. We went to sleep at one thirty a.m. with our bodies tired and our spirits very low.

The next morning, we discussed trying an experiment- not to take any pain medication and see if I stopped throwing up. This would not be an easy experiment but I was desperate, running out of options, and willing to try anything to get this thing back on track.

Mom helped me do some easy exercise. Dad then got the commode from the garage. After I had my bowel movement, Dad put on plastic gloves, and started taking careful samples in three plastic tubes. He said, "I don't mind doing this. I call this working on a shit-cocktail." He was trying to find an element of humor in this grim situation. He then drove to the medical lab to drop off the samples.

By one thirty, Mom and Dad were loading me in the car. We were on our way to Jersey Central Physical Therapy (JCPT). We were full of anxiety because we had no idea whether the therapists there were any good. From my home, it would take a twenty-minute drive to Route 287, then ten minutes on 287, and another ten minutes on Route 27. JCPT was located in the same building where, years ago, the headquarters of Revlon was located.

Dad was nervous. We were late. What if they refused to see us? Once there, we did not find any empty parking spaces near the main building. Dad drove near the entrance, and put the car in park with the engine running. He ran to a security guard and asked how to go to JCPT. The guard saw me laboring out of the car and into the wheelchair. He walked to us, and said, "Let me take you there." Then he said to my dad, "See this handicapped parking? Just park there." He took us through the main hallway towards another building and showed us the entrance of JCPT.

As we were walking across the hall towards the receptionist, I thought my ankle movement was getting worse every day; the nerves in my right leg already seemed damaged. I knew we needed nothing short of a miracle worker.

I wondered if such a miracle worker worked at Jersey Central. It seemed that it wasn't very likely.

19   God Wanted a Climatic Chapter

As we walked across the hall at JCPT, we saw six treadmills at the far corner, seven bikes, six elliptical transports, various leg abduction and flexion exercise machines, and many upper body machines. Is this a therapy place or a gym? I was wondering. Across from the treadmill, four TVs were hanging on the ceiling. For a gym, this appeared to be a first rate place.

The front reception area was fairly big, with three people working behind the desk. I was asked to fill out a multitude of forms. Once I was finished, the receptionist said, "Let me call Reena." In a minute, a pretty Indian girl walked towards us. She looked way too young to be an experienced therapist. I estimated her age to be about mid twenties. She was a petite woman, with curly hair and sharp features. She flashed a professional smile and said, "Follow me." She took me to the back end of the hall. That is where all the therapists did their work. There were several therapy mats. She wanted to see if I could get onto a higher mat, but I could not. She took me to a low mat. Then she started measuring my joint movements. She used a goniometer to take measurements and then took meticulous notes.

By this time, it was close to half an hour into the appointment and we only had a forty-five minute session. Mom and Dad looked worried. They were already losing faith in this place. "All they are doing is filling up the billable hours!" Dad thought.

"If they make their money doing paperwork, they can't be good," thought Mom. Our hope that this place would make a difference for us was getting shattered.

But then, Reena asked me to lie down on the bed and the therapy began. As I was lying on my back, she stood in front of me, lifted my right leg, and straightened it at the knee. She then pulled the leg up until it almost made a ninety-degree angle with my body. Then she put her body weight on my ankle to bring it down to the neutral position. Boy, did that hurt! But there was a confident rhythm in the way Reena was doing this. I was in pain yet happy. I laughingly said, "The only reason you can hurt me like this is because you're so pretty."

She smiled, only a bit, and then said, "Flattery won't work with me, Mister," and pushed my ankle back into neutral. Mom and Dad were standing a few feet away from me and heard our exchange. I saw Dad grab Mom's hand and take her aside.

He then whispered to her, "This therapist seems to know what she's doing. Akash also seems to have good chemistry with her. Can we make a second appointment for this evening?"

"Today?" Mom asked.

"Yes, we have been having difficulty motivating Akash. By coming here, at least we can add an hour of good exercise."

Mom knew things had to get better for me fast or else we would not be able to start the lengthening. She quickly walked to the receptionist desk and started working on them. She got one appointment that evening and two more for the next day.

Reena worked on me expertly. She did more things to my legs in one session than Susan had done in two weeks. The forty-five minute session lasted for two hours. We thought they would charge us for multiple sessions, but they did not. It was their standard fee of $45. In a single session, I felt that my ankle movement had already improved.

We left JCPT at four fifteen. I was feeling hungry after many days and felt like having falafel. We stopped by at Jerusalem Restaurant and picked up falafels for all of us. We were in a good mood as we drove home. We seemed to have found a good therapist and for the first time in a while, I felt hungry. The inside of the car was filled with the sweet smell of humus, falafels, and Baba Ghanoush. The falafel tasted very good. I finished one and wondered if I should stop, but I was feeling hungry after a long time. I had a second one.

Before we went back for our second session with Jersey Central, Mom still had to do pin care. That always took a solid hour. So I went from a pleasant falafel at the dinner table to painful pin care in my bed. Only Mom was going to take me for the second session, and Dad was going to stay home and send Dr. Rozbruch an e-mail update. At six forty-five p.m., I moved from the bed to the wheelchair. Mom started the car, and Dad was rolling the wheelchair down the ramp in the garage.

I turned my head and said "The stomach does not feel good, Dad."

He didn't say anything for a few seconds, and then said, "I'm coming with you." Dad went back in the kitchen and got a plastic garbage bag and a vomit tray. As he sat next to me, he said, "It's probably only gas; don't worry about it. Don't even think about throwing up." I wondered how I could not think about it, if he was sitting next to me with a vomit tray in his hand!

Five minutes into the ride, I burped. That was a good sign. There was a sense of relief in all three of us. Maybe it was gas after all.

But it wasn't. We had stopped to get gas. I said to Dad, "Quick give me the vomit tray." For the next five minutes, every last drop from my stomach came out. It was a painful vomit. At the end of it, I was tired and exhausted. I had tears in my eyes. Mom and Dad were speechless. I hadn't taken a pain medication all day. We thought that would do the trick. But that theory was busted.

Mom said, "Let me call JCPT and cancel your session."

"No, I can handle it," I said.

Dad said, "This was a pretty bad vomit. You look tired and ex-hausted- how can you exercise for an hour?"

In the opening scene of *Mrs. Doubtfire*, Robin Williams impersonates Gandhi and says a line. I said the same line to Dad, with the same Gandhi accent. I said, "*I have got to do what I have got to do.*" That eased the ten-sion in the car. Mom drove another half an hour and we were at Jersey Central. The handicapped parking spot was one hundred feet away from the entrance. As per our precise routine, Dad would take the wheelchair out of the trunk, open it, and position it near the door. I would then slide my body to the edge of the car seat and put both feet on the ground. The armrest of the wheelchair had already been lifted up. I then would slide from the car seat to the wheelchair. Then Mom or Dad would wheel me down the long walkway and to the front entrance.

Once inside, Mom told Reena what happened on the way over. Reena, with a concerned look, asked me, "Hey buddy, are you sure you can go through with this?"

I said, "Yes."

But my face looked pale and tired. Reena suggested that I lie down for five minutes before starting. Who in their right mind, after such a violent vomit, would go through severe exercise on the body parts that have been broken in two and had screws and bolts sticking into them?

But I knew that I had no other choice.

Reena did not push me as much in the evening as she had in the af-ternoon. My ankle and knee motion seemed to be getting ever so slightly better. We left JCPT at nine. At home, I ate barely four spoons of spaghetti. And then we waited. Would it stay in? By ten, the food was still in. We were still sitting at the kitchen table.

Suddenly I was feeling a sense of hopelessness. I was not sure anymore whether this was a mere nightmare. Maybe I would wake up and would be in my dormitory in Drexel. I was getting angry. I said, "I can't take it anymore." Mom looked at me with a look of despair. I looked at Dad, and then stared at the kitchen table. I shook my head, "I did not know it would be this hard."

The lengthening had stopped since the previous day and Dr. Rozbruch wasn't likely to let me continue lengthening. Mom and Dad were hoping that the therapy at JCPT would fix this problem and the lengthening would start again. I didn't share their optimism. "I don't know. I just don't know." I was repeating myself. Auntie was standing near the sink, listening to our conversation. Everyone in the room knew that we were running out of options.

We had carefully planned every aspect of this surgery for the last two years, and it wasn't supposed to end like this. The therapy at JCPT was nothing short of torture. If I did not go through with it, the lengthening would stop, but if I went through with it, there was no guarantee that Rozbruch would allow the lengthening to continue. In that case, going through such torture would go to waste. The uncertainty of what lay ahead was very painful. There was one way to reduce anxiety and remove uncertainty. *Take the damn rings off now!* Then I would not have to worry any more whether I could improve my ankle motion or not.

I looked at Dad and said, "I want these frames taken out *right now!*" And then I put my head on the kitchen table and started weeping. I was crying uncontrollably. Mom got up and hugged me. She started sobbing. I motioned Dad to come to me. He held Mom and me. For the next five minutes, we cried tears of helplessness. I looked back. Auntie was standing near the sink, her face covered with her hands, tears rolling down her cheeks.

But then Dad composed himself. He got up, got the camcorder out from the camera cabinet, and turned it on. He said, "Akash, can you move your chair back a little? I want you to take my movie." He said, "I'm going to summarize the events of the last two days. Let us keep a record of what is happening"

Taking a movie was not Mom's thing, so I knew I had to compose myself. I stopped sobbing, wiped my tears, turned on the camera, put Dad in the center of the frame, and said, "Go."

"This has been a very tough two days for our Shukla family," Dad said in a crackling voice. He spoke haltingly at times, holding back tears. He spoke with conviction. He summarized the events of the last two days: the continuous vomit since the last ten days, the bad news from Dr. Rozbruch, finding JCPT, and throwing up on the way to see them. He then summarized the difficult situation about how our options were dwindling.

This had a surprising effect on me. It was like when a hiker is lost in the woods and somebody lifts him up in a helicopter and lets the hiker get a birds-eye view of his surroundings. By the time Dad finished, there was a little less gloom in the room and I was determined to make this thing work.

On Wednesday, November 24, I had two appointments at Jersey Central- one in the morning and one in the evening. The evening session was going to be a pool therapy. When you are in the water, you don't feel as much weight, and therefore 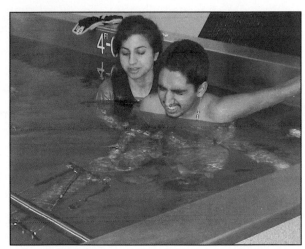 you can do some movements that otherwise you could not. The screws and pins going in my body would ooze on a daily basis. Wouldn't the wounds get infected by exposing them to pool water? I wondered. Alex Ivashenko, the owner and the chief PT, explained to Mom how the water was purified 100 percent and that there was no chance of getting an infection.

Alex was a tall guy, maybe in his early forties, but looked younger. He looked like a research scientist or a medical doctor. He spoke with confidence and authority. He had a master's degree in physical therapy and was working on his PhD.

Each one-hour session at JCPT took an additional two hours to get us there and back. If we did this twice a day, we would spend six hours every day for my physical therapy. Not just me, but my mom and dad would have to spend this time. On Wednesday, both Mom and Dad decided to become members at the gym at JCPT. That way, while I was getting physical therapy, they would be exercising on the treadmill, bike, elliptical transport, and the other weight machines. We had made this whole thing a family project.

Dad got up early on Wednesday and started composing a letter to Dr. Rozbruch. We were convinced that the therapy I was receiving at JCPT had already improved my ankle motion somewhat. We also thought that I was ready to start distraction again. But unless we correctly communicated that to Dr. Rozbruch, and unless he was convinced, he would not give us the go-ahead to restart the lengthening. Dad selected every word carefully. He would write a paragraph and then re-write it. We needed to convince Dr. Rozbruch to restart the lengthening.

Mom and I had to leave for therapy at noon. Dad was still putting the finishing touches on the letter and said he would e-mail it by noon. I read the draft and made a few suggestions. Mom looked at it and thought it was good as it was. This was an important document. It could revive the project that had come to a sudden halt. Even though some of the details in the letter have already been explained in my previous chapter, I have included the letter in it's entirety so that the reader can get a true flavor of the details and passion in the letter.

From: Shukla Meena & Rahul

Sent: Wednesday, November 24, 2004 12:09 PM

To: 'Rozbruch, S. Robert MD'

Cc: 'wagnerp@hss.edu';

Subject: A rather long letter: Please pardon so many details.

Hello Dr. Rozbruch,

It has been two very tough days since we left your office. Before I give you the update on specific items, I just wanted to share with you how devastated all of us are with this sudden turn of events. Akash's stomach problems came unexpectedly. We do not know how many more days or even weeks it may take before the vomiting and nausea situation is resolved. Not a single full meal in fifteen days has stayed in his system. That caused an extreme weakness, which in turn slowed his exercise routine, which probably contributed to the stiffening of his knee and ankle.

We had agonized over the pros and cons of this surgery for the last three years. We carefully planned every detail for the last six months. Akash has invested a whole academic year on this. Meena and I have put our lives on hold. We are stunned at the thought of stopping at thirty-six millimeters. We are hoping that you can figure out a way to keep this "alive" while the other doctors investigate what is happening with his stomach- and while the new therapists work at gaining his ankle movement back. It would be a terrible blow to us if we had to stop prematurely.

Here is an update:

(We included details on my vomits and the visit to Dr. Goyal. The letter then continued about JCPT.)

Physical Therapy: We have switched to Jersey Physical Therapy Center in Edison, NJ. We got their number from your office. The therapists are very knowledgeable, motivated, pleasant, and persuasive. Akash had a first session yesterday afternoon. We saw a substantial progress in the first session. We made a second appointment for last night. It was on our way to the second appointment when Akash emptied out his falafels. Even then, he wanted to do the second session and did vigorous exercise for ninety minutes.

Ankle/Knee Movement: From the afternoon session to the evening session at Jersey Therapy Center, we saw a tremendous improvement (picture attached). The ankle that was very stiff in your office comes to almost 95 to 98 degrees. I think it will be at 90 degrees within a few more days. Two days ago, he could not put much weight on his feet. By last night, he was walking fifteen steps. I cannot say 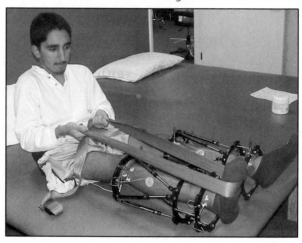 enough nice things about the therapist, Reena Sehgal, and her colleagues. We have booked two sessions today, two on Friday, and two on Saturday. I think you will see a marked improvement next time you see Akash.

Nerve Stretching: When you held Akash's knee straight and pushed the right ankle, he had complained about a severe burning sensation in three of his toes on his right foot. Since then that sensation has subsided, but is not completely gone. During the two sessions he had at Jersey Therapy (during most of the stretches of the ankle), he did not feel any burning sensations in those toes. There were two times when he felt the tingling sensation but he said it was much less than what he felt in your office. I am hoping that by the time we make it back to your office, that sensation will be completely gone. I know you were most concerned about that more than anything else.

Pin Pain: Akash feels more severe pain on certain pins: On the left leg, near the knee, two pins on the right side give him extreme pain. He says it feels like the pins are pinching a nerve. On the right leg, near the ankle, one pin has similar pain. There is no objective way to gauge whether the pain is more or less than what it has been all along.

Pin Condition: Pins continue to look good. No further redness or puffiness.

Pain Management: It seems that the new pain medication, Hydromorphine, does not work on Akash's pain as well as Vicodin did. Of course, there are no objective ways to test this hypothesis. The reason for switching from Vicodin to Darvoset to Hydromorphine was to alleviate the nausea and vomiting. Since vomiting has continued anyway, I am wondering if it will be okay to try Vicodin again. I am sending a copy of this e-mail to Dr. Wagner, and I will contact him to see if he wants to make any adjustment in the pain medicine.

Akash's Frame of Mind: Akash is extremely depressed with the turn of events. The constant nausea has tired him emotionally. With medication coming out during vomit, the pin pain is becoming more severe. Prior to the stomach episodes, Akash handled his pain a lot better and was in much more positive frame of mind. In the last five days, he is losing his resolve. He cannot wait till the fixators are gone. (He wants to burn them and melt them!) He still wants to continue the lengthening- and may even consider the tissue release procedure- but he is terrified at the idea of additional pins in his ankle. I have promised him that we will NOT consider the option of additional rings on his ankle.

Dr. Rozbruch, Akash has shown extraordinary courage in wanting to go through with this surgery. I hope you can show us a way where his sacrifice and his sufferings do not go unrewarded and that he can continue at least for another fourteen millimeters. I know he would not have opted for this surgery if he had known that he could gain only an inch and a half out of it.

I will keep you up to date on the findings of Dr. Goyal. I hope Akash does not have gallstones or some other unexpected stomach problems. If he does, I hope you can figure out a way to keep this matter on hold until we fix all other things.

    -Rahul

Dad sent the letter at 12:09 p.m. By then, Mom and I had left for JCPT. Mom was very concerned that I would miss therapy the next day because of the Thanksgiving holiday and then again on Sunday when JCPT was closed. Once I started my therapy with Reena, Mom went and talked to Alex. "Is there any way we can get therapy on Sunday?" she asked.

"Sunday we are closed," said Alex. Mom explained to Alex how this was the most critical phase of the surgery and unless my motion got back to normal and my nerve pain went away, the doctor would stop the lengthening for good. Alex said, "Reena is taking Friday off. You better go to the reception desk and make your appointments for Friday and Saturday quickly."

Alex had a staff of some fourteen people. Reena, Jennifer, Maureen, and Jaime were all trained and licensed physical therapists. So, of course, was Alex. We would not mind getting a few sessions with him. But he was the big boss and we weren't sure whether he himself did any therapy. Mom thought it would be nice to mix things up between Alex and Reena. Reena was focused and methodical but Alex had twenty years of experience and he was going for his PhD. How much more qualified a person could we find to work with me?

Mom walked to the receptionist; in three short days, everyone at JCPT had become very friendly with us. They had all heard about our challenges, were impressed with my courage and my parents' commitment, and they all had secretly started rooting for me. Mom talked to Judy at the receptionist's desk and said, "We have to have two appointments on Friday. Can we do both of them with Alex?"

"That's nearly impossible," said Judy, "but I can give you one in the afternoon with Alex. He is completely booked the rest of the day." At that time, Alex was walking by. Mom stopped him and asked, "Why don't you work with Akash prior to your first appointment Friday morning?" Alex thought for a second and then said, "Can you be here at seven thirty a.m.?" Without hesitating for a second, Mom said, "Yes we can." She then said, "How about Sunday?"

Alex said, "I know how important this is to you." He thought for a minute. Then he said, "I will come to open the office and work with Akash myself. But I'll have to charge you one hundred and fifty dollars for that session." When the head therapist, on his day off, drives one hour, opens this huge place just for you, and works with you for an hour, one hundred and fifty dollars seems like a very good bargain. Mom quickly called Dad at home and asked for his opinion.

Dad had developed a good clarity about the situation. He said, "This project is going to cost us close to $200,000. For that, Akash will gain between two to two and a half inches. That is almost $100,000 an inch. If we are forced to stop now, Akash will lose half an inch. That is equivalent to $50,000. If we spend an additional $5,000 for extra therapy and salvage this half an inch, that will be the equivalent of buying $50,000 for a mere $5,000." Mom quickly gave the go-ahead to Alex for the Sunday session.

Unlike the previous evening, Reena pushed me very hard. She had a no-nonsense approach. She would only chuckle and never laugh at my jokes. She was pretty, charming, and very focused. If you *had* to allow someone to inflict such horrendous pain on you, you could not find a better person. I allowed her to push me far beyond what I thought I was capable of. On our way home, I was very tired and exhausted. But the day was not over- not by a long shot. I knew that once I went home, ate, and did pin care, I would be ready for my return trip to JCPT.

When we reached home and Dad heard the garage door open, he ran to the garage and started helping me out of the car and into the house. He had a relaxed smile on his face. He looked at us and gave a double thumbs-up sign.

"What happened?" I asked.

"We heard from Dr. Rozbruch," he said

"Already?" I asked.

"Yes," he said. "We can start a half millimeter distraction as of tomorrow."

There was a great sigh of relief. Wow. It was back on again! I quickly wheeled myself over to the computer to read Dr. Rozbruch's e-mail response. As usual, it was short, and to the point.

```
Thanks for the update. Sounds positive other
than the GI situation. Start the lengthening on
Fri at three struts per day. Keep pushing the
PT.

Happy Thanksgiving.

S. Robert Rozbruch, MD
```

The dark clouds of the last three days were slowly lifting away. What seemed hopeless three days ago was back on track again.

Two days ago, when my spirits were down in the dumps, Dad sat down next to me and said, "Look at it this way. If you overcome this, you will have a climactic chapter in your book. Maybe that is why God is doing this to you."

And so this is that climactic chapter.

20   It Is Getting Bleaker

We could have started turning the nuts on the frame on the evening of November 24, but we collectively decided to start the process the next day. My stomach had not settled yet and I was throwing up almost every day. I had lost ten pounds in the last fifteen days. All of us were thrilled that the process was back on, but we also knew that this was only a provisional reprieve. We were scheduled to see Dr. Rozbruch in four days, on November 29. At that time, he would decide whether the lengthening could continue or whether it should be stopped.

My room had started to look like a war situation room. Dad was searching for solutions to my stomach problem on the internet. Could it be that all the antibiotics I'd taken had killed off the good bacteria in the colon, created an imbalance, and that was why I'd been throwing up? Dad told me yogurt replaces these bacteria. He wanted to put me on "yogurt therapy." I absolutely hated yogurt.

Mom wanted to test the theory that pain medication was the culprit. On November 24 and November 25, I took only Tylenol to control my pain. That was not an easy experiment.

Dad also hung a second board next to the medicine and exercise schedule board. Mom and Dad listed my complete daily activities-what time I woke up, what time I went to the bathroom, what time I had breakfast and what I ate. At night, just before we went to sleep, Dad would take a picture of each board so that we had a record of every-thing that happened on that day. What was happening to me was a mystery, and if we looked at enough

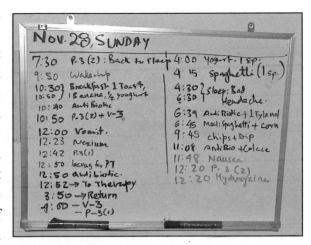

clues, we should be able to get to the bottom of it.

On Thanksgiving, I got up at nine thirty and sat down for break-fast. I had half a bagel, cereal, and a banana. I was afraid to eat. Even though the doctor had given an okay for lengthening, we had not found a solution to my stomach problems. Things looked pretty bleak. I was wondering, "Do I have anything to be thankful for?" A series of bad things, one after the other, was happening. Why would I be thankful? I wondered. But then I thought, God did bring Jersey Central into our life. Reena was an expert therapist, and Alex seemed very knowledge-able about my procedure. Ever since the surgery, I had been getting countless phone calls from friends and family from all over the world. Relatives and friends called from India, Australia, England, Canada, and from all over the United States. My uncle, aunt, cousin, and their families in New Jersey were always looking after me. After I got back from the hospital, there was a constant flow of people who came to see me.

As for good luck, we did find many great doctors. Dr. Rozbruch was one of the authorities when it came to limb lengthening surgery. Dr. MacKenzie was a compassionate doctor who treated me with kindness. Dr. Wagner, the pain specialist, was taking a keen interest in finding a solution to my sickness. Dr. Goyal was an expert in gastroin-testinal matters. Dr. Bharti Shah, my childhood pediatrician, was calling every day and giving us guidance. Granted, a few things with my health were screwed up now, but at the same time, God had sent so many experts into my life to help me solve my problems. And of course, I had a pair of parents like nobody else in the world. So, I said to myself, come to think of it, I do have a lot to be thankful for on this Thanksgiving Day.

I was trying to feel good about my situation by thinking about all of those things. That feeling did not last too long. I threw up at three in the afternoon. Dad had a long face. Every one of his theories, which made a lot of sense in the beginning, ended up being incorrect. He said, "Don't worry, we will figure this out." I could see that he was fighting back tears. He didn't want to cry in front of me and said, "I need to go for a ride."

When he came back forty-five minutes later, he had lost his voice. He must have cried his heart out in the car. He said in a soft, crackly tone to Mom, "Let's get Akash ready; we are going to the temple." He then turned to me, "We have sought the advice of the top medical experts in the world. Now it is time that we seek guidance from a higher authority." We were not a particularly religious family. My dad always jokingly said, "God has the whole universe to look after. Don't go knocking on his door unless you have an urgent problem. Don't call him just to say good morning. That may tie up his line for somebody else who really needs to talk to him."

When I was four months old, in 1986, my mom and dad took me to India. They were thrilled with my arrival and they wanted to share that joy with my grandparents and all the other relatives in India. Shortly after we got there, I got a bad stomach virus. I had a very high fever, followed by severe diarrhea. The pediatrician in the city, Surendranagar, examined me and shook his head. "This doesn't look good," he said. "Why don't you take him to Ahmedabad?"

Ahmedabad is the largest city in the state where my grandparents lived. There were many expert medical doctors in that city. Once we got to Ahmedabad, my parents enlisted one of the top doctors to look after me. The doctor said, "We will try to save your son!" My parents were stunned and absolutely frightened. I had a fever of 104 degrees. "Why did we bring him to India at this young age?" they kept lamenting. They would sit next to my bed all night, holding my hand. That was their way of continuously checking my temperature.

In four days, I got better. Dad said, "I'll have to go make a trip to my college city, Bhavnagar." There was a temple of Lord Shiva on a hilltop. When Dad was a mechanical engineering student and was competing in many debating competitions, he would make a promise that if God let him win this debate, he would take a ceremonial coconut to express his gratitude. That particular God had been responsive to Dad's gifts. So, many years later, sitting next to my bed in Ahmedabad, Dad made a similar pledge. "When Akash gets better, I will go to that temple and take a holy coconut."

Once we went back from Ahmedabad to Surendranagar, Dad was talking with our family friend, a brilliant surgeon, Dr. Kharod. Dad said to Dr. Kharod, "Ordinarily, I'm a logical person and do not believe in any superstition. I am embarrassed that I resorted to this. But a promise is a promise. Tomorrow I have to go to Bhavnagar."

Dr. Kharod said, "Don't be so hard on yourself. It would have been wrong to resort to prayer if you had neglected to first get the top medical attention. But after doing everything medically that you could, there is nothing wrong in asking for divine intervention." Dr. Kharod then said, *"When logic ends, faith begins."*

Such was the case with my situation in 2004. We had contacted every top expert in the field, tried every anti-nausea medication known to mankind. We tried to analyze the cause of the vomit. But logic had failed us. It was time now to turn to faith.

Mom helped me get ready. When the rest of our extended family heard that we were going to the temple, they all said they would meet us there. They knew we were at the end of our rope. They wanted to show their support and say a prayer for me. My vomit had to stop, my ankle motion had to return to normal, and the nerve pain had to go away. Only then could we continue the distraction. We needed divine help from God on all these matters.

Dad said to Mom, "You and I are 'take-charge' people. We think we can take care of everything. We thought we would help Akash change his height because we are so smart and we can do anything. I think God is not happy with that kind of arrogance. We need to go to the temple and ask for forgiveness. We will promise we will never be arrogant again. We know that God, and not we, can make things happen. We will plead that he does not punish our son for our arrogance."

Dad looked like he was ready for a nervous breakdown. Mom gave him a hug and said, "Rahul, everything will work out. Don't lose your faith."

The drive to the Bridgewater Temple took us thirty minutes. It took another fifteen minutes to get me into the wheelchair, take me through the elevator, and up on the main hall. We purchased the Archna, just as we had done the day before my surgery on September 23. We stood in front of God Venkateswara. There were lots of people in the temple and we were scared that someone might bump into my frames. If that happened, and if I fell off the chair and damaged the bone at the point of incision, then that would be another catastrophe. Mom unfolded the walker and put it in front of my wheelchair, protecting my legs. The priest came and stood in front of us. He took the plate of Archna from Mom's hands. The priest looked at me in the wheelchair. He saw the pain on my face and tears in Mom's eyes. He figured out that we needed God's help. He asked Mom, "What is your gotra?"

"Darlabh," said Mom.

The priest knew this prayer was for me, so he turned to me and asked for my name. "Akash," I told him. He then said his prayer in Sanskrit, right then and there, using my name in the prayer. He then turned to Dad, and asked his name. Dad was so overcome with emotion that he could not say his name at first.

Then we all prayed. I said, "God, I am losing my resolve. I started this painful journey thinking you would look after me. Please help me."

After the prayer, we made our usual rounds to all of the gods. Dad went around the statues of the nine planets by himself, on my behalf. Dad then turned to Mom and said, "We have to pray to Ganpati."

Ganpati is the son of Shiva. He has a human body and an elephant's head. A month ago, our family friends Uncle Maruti and Aunt Rajni had come to see me. Uncle Maruti had reminded Dad that Ganpati is "*Vighnahari.*" That, in Sanskrit, meant "One who removes your difficulties." Dad wanted all three of us to say a special prayer to Ganpati.

My uncle had brought his three-year-old daughter, and my cousin had brought his three daughters, twin three-year-olds, and a one-year-old. The kids gave me a hug. My relatives' faces all showed tremendous concern. Their presence in the temple gave me much needed strength. We went downstairs to the temple cafeteria. I was feeling hungry. I first had one serving of idli (rice cakes). I felt like a second one. I looked at Mom and Dad. Mom read the plea on my face. I was hungry. Should I venture a second one? Without saying a word, Mom got up and got me a second serving. They thought that food eaten in God's place would stay in.

The idlis did stay in.

On our way home, we felt that the visit to the temple had created some tranquility in all of us. Dad said he had sent his apologies. Mom had said her prayers. I had said my prayers. We needed a break. We needed divine help.

Would God send help our way?

21   God Listened to Our Prayers

The day after Thanksgiving, I woke up at three in the morning with extreme pain in my entire lower body. I took one Hydromorphine, one Tylenol, and one anti-nausea medicine, Trimthrobcuz, and then went back to sleep. I got up at six forty-five and took another pain medication. I had a seven thirty appointment with Alex. Experience had taught me that if I took pain medication an hour before my appointment, then I was better able to withstand the forced flexion for my knees and ankles. Mom, Dad, and I got in the car and were on our way to JCPT. The roads had spotty ice patches. On River Road, our car started skidding on an ice patch. That was a bit scary. Mom said, "We don't need any more crises in our life."

Once at JCPT, Alex took me to the back and started working on me. Mom and Dad stayed with me for a few minutes and then went to the far end of the room some thirty feet away to start their exercises.

Alex started working on my ankle flexion. He pushed much harder than Reena used to. I was making loud sighs of pain. I told him it was hurting way too much. When he pushed the ankle, it would put pressure on the pins above the ankle. That caused the pins to radiate with pain. "I know it hurts, but trust me, I know what I'm doing," he said.

At times, I thought I was going to pass out from the pain. Alex started asking me if I had heard any good jokes lately. What a consummate professional Alex was. He knew that if I tried to remember and tell him a joke, it would take my mind off the pain he was putting me through. I told him, "Bob Smith recently purchased a very expensive hearing aid. Bob was telling his friend, 'I bought this top of the line, very expensive hearing aid.' His friend asked, 'What kind is it?' 'Half past four,' said Bob."

Alex was laughing hard. He then asked me about my plans for college.

"I have been accepted into Drexel University in Philadelphia. I am going to study mechanical engineering," I told him.

"Mechanical engineering! What made you choose that?"

"I think engineering teaches you how things work. That in turn makes you good at everything else. Whether you want to be a surgeon or a lawyer, learning mechanical engineering first wouldn't hurt."

"That's interesting," said Alex.

"Also, some of the smartest people in the world have studied mechanical engineering," I said with a chuckle, "That's what my dad keeps telling me."

"I guess your dad is a mechanical engineer," Alex said.

"How did you ever guess?" I joked.

"What does he do?" Alex asked me.

"He owns a manufacturing company in Piscataway. We make automotive and aircraft parts. Ours is one of the oldest manufacturing companies in the United States. It was founded in 1844."

"What's the name of your company?" Alex asked.

"S.S. White Technologies."

"Wait a minute." He stopped mid-stretch. He looked at me inquisitively, and asked, "Do you guys know Doug and Cathy Shipman?"

"Surely!" I said, "Mr. Shipman is my dad's best friend, and he was our next-door neighbor. When I grew up, I jokingly called him Doug

Kaka. Kaka by the way," I told Alex, "means uncle in Gujarati, my dad's mother tongue."

"Wow," said Alex. "I think I know your dad. My wife, Caroline, grew up in the same neighborhood as Doug. We have known Doug and Cathy ever since childhood. We still are the best of friends. As a matter of fact, I *met* your dad many years ago."

I looked at the far end of the room. Dad, in his orange and black sweatshirt, was running on the treadmill. I kept motioning him to come to me. After several seconds, he saw me. He stopped the treadmill and started walking, almost running, towards me. He had a worried look on his face. He thought I was about to throw up. "What?" he asked.

"Dad, Alex thinks he has met you before."

Dad looked at Alex and tried to jog his memory. "When?" asked Dad.

"You're friends with Doug?" asked Alex.

"Who- Doug Shipman?"

"Yes. Doug and Cathy. I'm Doug's close friend. I think I met you in 1984."

Of course he had! Mom and Dad had moved to a new development in 1981. Their next-door neighbors were Doug and Cathy. They were a very friendly, bright, and driven couple. What started as a neighborly acquaintance became a friendship that would last a lifetime. Once Dad got to know Doug, he thought Doug was one of the smartest engineers he had ever met. Just at that time, in 1982, Dad was promoted to Director of Research and Development position at S.S. White. Dad talked Doug into working for him. Together, they did a lot of exciting things and had a lot of fun. On the weekends, they used to sit out in the backyard and drink wine coolers together.

In 1984, they started doing automation work using computers. They would take an electrical signal, convert it into a digital signal, read it through the RS232 of a computer, and have the computer turn on or off appropriate devices. In 1984, this was breakthrough technology.

My dad and Mr. Shipman were ready to quit their jobs at S.S. White and start their own process-automation company. They could computerize many processes that, in 1984, were not yet computerized. For instance, the stress test to evaluate a heart condition was one of the projects they were working on. Mr. Shipman told Dad, "Two of my best friends are physical therapists. They have a very successful practice. Can we design some instruments for them, and also get involved with them in some business ventures?"

So in 1984, Mr. Shipman and Dad had lunch with these two young physical therapists- Mr. Shipman's two best friends. One was named Rick and the second . . . was named Alex. The same Alex who, in 2004 at Jersey Central Physical Therapy, was working on my ankle.

What a small world. Dad shook hands with Alex. Suddenly, there was an intimate bond between us and him. Alex said to Dad, "I think my wife also knows you." Caroline, a slender, tall, and pretty woman, helped Alex run the business and helped run the front desk.

To understand our connection with Caroline, let me continue with the S.S. White story. Dad decided not to go ahead with the new process-automation company. Mr. Shipman left S.S. White in 1986, and created his own successful process-automation company. Destiny had big things in store for Dad, too. Through some unique twists of events, Dad ended up buying S.S. White Technologies from Pennwalt Corporation. Dad and Mr. Shipman remained best friends, and took a keen interest in each other's business.

By 1993, Mr. Shipman had sold his company and was in-between businesses. Dad's company needed to design brand new winding machines. Dad still believed that Doug Shipman was the brightest engineer he had ever met. So again Dad talked Mr. Shipman into coming to work for S.S. White, to run the engineering department and design and build new winding machines. The new winding machines were complex devices, forty feet long, needing many machined metal parts. Mr. Shipman knew this expert machinist who owned a machine shop in Edison, New Jersey. His name was Al Young and he owned Edison Machine Tools. Al came to Dad's company many times, worked closely with Mr. Shipman in making numerous parts for Dad's company, and also met Dad several times.

On that November 26 morning, Alex asked Dad, "Do you remember Al Young?"

Dad said, "Yeah. He owned Edison Machine Tools. He did a lot of work for my company."

Alex said, "My wife, Caroline, is Al's daughter. She too knows you very well."

On our way back home, Mom, Dad, and I could not stop talking about this tremendous coincidence. Alex seemed to be at the top of his game. He seemed to have made a personal commitment to see that I got all the help I needed. Now, he turned out to be the best friend of our best friend. Yesterday, it seemed that logic had ended, and we had to turn to faith when we went to the temple and asked for God's help.

As our car was riding back on Route 287 from Jersey Central to our home, the three of us felt that God had intervened, listened to our prayers, and sent Alex , Caroline, and Reena to our rescue.

22   The Tough Times Continue

On our way back from JCPT, Mom and Dad kept talking about this wonderful break. I was a little quiet. My stomach was not feeling good. I did not want to talk about it and dampen the uplifting mood Mom and Dad were in. We got home at 9:20 a.m. I took one Nexium, a pill that can heal erosion in the esophagus. Then I took a short nap. When I got up, I had a light breakfast of one waffle and one banana. My allergies were acting up, so I took one Hydroxezine. At 11:20 a.m., I took one more pain medication.

At 11:50 a.m., the banana and the waffle came out.

We were all heartbroken. With all the other good things happening and the temple idli staying in last night, we had hoped that the vomit problem was resolved. It was not. Since the pain medication probably came out with rest of the stomach contents, I took one more pain medication at 12:40 p.m. Throwing up for the last two weeks had made me very weak. I had absolutely no desire to put food in my mouth. Mom and Dad told me one more time that even if I threw up, I still had to eat. I needed energy to exercise; I also needed food in my body so the new bone could form. I ate two Munchkins. At one thirty, I took the anti-nausea medication. I was preparing myself to eat lunch.

Dad said, "We need a new hypothesis about the cause of the vomit. We have to solve this puzzle." He started writing on the dry erase board all the different dates and times of my vomits. He also wrote the times of food and medication intake for each date. Every time I threw up, it was within ninety to a hundred and twenty minutes after eating. Other than that, there was no pattern at all. Dad said, "There seems to be no correlation with what you eat. What does that mean? How come there is no correlation?" We did not know the answer.

Just then, Rajen Uncle and Neha Auntie came to see me. I was feeling hungry, which was a good sign. Normally I only had one vomit a day, which was already behind me. I was ready to venture another meal. We got two pies of pizza from Dominoes. I had two slices of pizza at two thirty. As we were preparing to leave for our four o'clock therapy appointment, I said to Dad, "I feel like I'm going to throw up."

Uncle Rajen said, "Maybe it's just gas. Don't worry about it. Think positive."

Dad had a gloomy look on his face. He stared at the ceiling for a second, then turned to Rajen Uncle and said, "Every time Akash said he was going to throw up, he did." As usual, the vomit tray and the vomit bag was prepared and positioned properly in the car. Once on our way to JCPT, I burped twice. They were loud burps. It was a rare time in my life that loud burps brought tremendous joy. Maybe it was gas after all.

Alex's wife, Caroline, greeted us at the reception desk at JCPT. She told my dad how her dad remembered him very well. As Dad was talking to Caroline, Mom and I proceeded to meet Alex. I transferred from the wheelchair to the low mat. Alex positioned himself on the stool. He put his hands on my ankle. I looked helplessly at Mom. "Mom," I said, "Can you give me the vomit tray?"

There was a look of defeat on her face. She could not believe this was happening. She quickly held the vomit tray under my mouth. I started throwing up. Mom yelled Dad's name. Dad was talking with Caroline. He turned towards us and saw Mom holding the pink tray, and me emptying my stomach into it. He came running. I continued to throw up as I stared helplessly at Dad. I don't think that there was a single drop left in my stomach. Alex and the other therapists and aides looked at me sympathetically. There was a stunned silence in the room.

Then I started shivering. My chin was chattering and my body was shaking. Alex helped me lie down and said to one of his aids, "Justin, get me a blanket- quickly." He covered me with a blanket. Mom and Dad were stroking my forehead. Alex looked at them reassuringly and said, "Let him take rest for a few minutes. Everything will be all right. We'll start working after a few minutes."

Mom looked at my shivering body, then turned towards Dad and said in a pleading voice, "How can he go on like this?" Tears were rolling down her cheeks. She said again, "Rahul, how can he go on like this? He's in no shape to go through this exercise."

I somehow knew that for me, this was now or never. I said, "Mom, let me rest for a while. I will be all right." They both sat next to me while I took a half an hour nap.

When I opened my eyes, Alex was standing at my feet. He said, "Are you ready now?"

"Let's do it," I said.

He started his therapy a little gentler than normal, but he took it to full speed in no time. Amazingly, my ankle motion was getting back to normal. It was almost back to where it was before I had started throwing up on November 10. Also, when Alex pushed my ankle to neutral, there was no longer the burning sensation in my toes.

On our way back home, we stopped by A&P and bought many flavors of yogurt. It was time for a different hypothesis. Maybe it was not a stomach virus, but that my system was so irritated that we needed to settle it with easy-to-digest foods.

My days were filled with highs and lows. One moment everything looked hopeless, and then we would see a ray of hope. For example, when we found out about Alex's connection to Doug, we were thrilled.

Since then, I threw up twice. We were devastated. This afternoon, miraculously, Alex got my ankle flexion back to where it should have been. We were feeling pretty good about this. This feeling of optimism would not last too long.

We came home and Mom started doing pin care. The pins were hurting more than usual. At one point, I was making sighs of pain. Dad didn't have the stomach to handle the sight or the sound of all of this. During pin care, he would go to the room farthest from my room. That day, Mom suddenly started looking for Dad. This was never a good sign. She called Dad and said, "Take a look at this pin." Dad had done

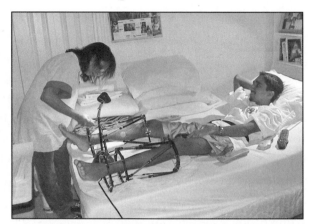

every other thing with me valiantly, but had avoided looking directly at the pin sites. Mom knew too well all about Dad's weak knees. For her to ask Dad to look at the pins would mean that something was not right, big time. A thick white substance was emerging from the pin site and depositing around it. In the early days, we used to think the pin was infected if the skin around the pin got all red, then the doctor said it was not infected unless there was pus coming out.

Well, this time, there was pus coming out. Dad took close-up pictures. He wanted to write a letter along with the pictures and e-mail it to Dr. Rozbruch. Just at that time, our family friend's three daughters-Bina, Jaine, Shilpa came to see me. They are kind, intelligent, and so very pretty. Dad referred to them as "Charlie's Angels." We all played the card game *PIT*. They posed with me for a lot of pictures. They brightened my mood. They left at eleven thirty p.m.

Mom checked the pin again. Some more white liquid had come out of that pin. Dad took another picture. Looking at his face, I knew this was serious. He said, "Every time we think it's an infection, Rozbruch says it is not. Maybe this time also, it is not." Mom suggested that Dad write to Dr. Rozbruch right away. He sat down to write a letter. Writing a letter to the doctor was not simple. We had to make sure it gave us desired results. Dad sent the letter to Dr. Rozbruch at two a.m. and then came to bed. As we all went to sleep, our hearts were sinking once again. Just when we had found an angel of a therapist to work with me, this infection could possibly put an end to this project.

When I woke up Saturday morning, I was in extreme pain. When I tried to move my ankle, I couldn't. I knew this was the most pain I had been in since the surgery. When I was in pain all the other times, I knew it would go away once I took the painkiller. There was something different about this pain. It was so severe I told Mom and Dad that they should take me to the hospital right away. Mom and Dad knew that if we went to the hospital, this project would come to an end. Dad said, "We should do that as a last resort." Deep down, all three of us knew that this project was coming to an end. I couldn't move my left ankle. Putting any weight on it was out of the question. It seemed certain that the lengthening would have to be put on hold. What had started again Friday would come to a stop one more time Saturday morning.

By ten a.m., Dad called Dr. Rozbruch's office and left a message. Rozbruch called back in ten minutes. Dad put him on speakerphone so all of us could talk to him. Dr. Rozbruch looked at the pictures as we were talking on the phone and said, "Yup, that is infected."

Dad asked if we should start the ten-day course of antibiotics. Dr. Rozbruch sounded a little annoyed. He said, "Why haven't you already started it?"

Dad said, "We wanted you to look at the pictures first."

Dr. Rozbruch said, "The next time you suspect an infection, don't wait for me to see it. Just start the antibiotic treatment."

Once we hung up, Mom and Dad were angry at themselves. Why had we not noticed it sooner? I reminded them that we saw the first sign of pus only last evening. Mom quickly gave me an antibiotic.

We had an eleven a.m. appointment at JCPT. To make it by eleven, we should have left at ten fifteen, but we were tied up on the phone with Dr. Rozbruch until ten forty-five. We knew that the appointment for the day was shot. Mom called JCPT, told Alex I had a possible infection, and that we couldn't make the eleven o'clock appointment. Alex said, "Finish everything you need to finish and come whenever you can." We weren't going to miss the appointment after all. God had indeed sent an angel to help us.

We left at eleven fifteen. I felt excruciating pain when I put any weight on my ankle. The pin with pus was hurting like crazy. The transfer from wheelchair to the car was very painful. I didn't think there would be much therapy today. I knew I wouldn't be able to take it. The reason for going, though, was so we could get Alex's professional opinion about the infection. Alex had seen this kind of procedure before. Rozbruch had only seen the pictures but Alex could see the actual site of the suspected infection.

We got at JCPT at noon. Alex did not think the pin was infected. He began working with me very gently. He knew how sore my right ankle was. Little by little, he started working the ankle. To my great surprise, by the time he was done, the movement of that ankle was back to ninety degrees. The ride home was a little less pessimistic.

Once we came home, after half an hour of rest, my exercise routine began again. Mom brought a towel, and I put it around my toes and pulled it towards me. Mom had incredible focus. She would encourage me, admire me, compliment me, and keep me focused. She would pull the towel to pull my foot. She would then count to thirty. This would be a tough exercise for someone in normal health; it would be a tough exercise even if you didn't have all these bolts and screws piercing your flesh and bone. It would be tough, even if there wasn't blood oozing from the wounds. For me it was like entering hell every thirty seconds. But I knew that if my ankle movement came back, I could reach my goal of two inches. If it did not, it would be a heartbreak. We were going to see Dr. Rozbruch two days later. It would all depend on what he said. If he said stop, that would be it. That fear kept me going.

That day, I was on a strict diet of stomach friendly items- items I would never have eaten if I was not so desperate. At eleven a.m., I had two slices of toast, half a can of yogurt, and half a banana for lunch; at two fifteen, one banana; at 3:10 p.m., half a can of yogurt and some potato chips; at four forty-five p.m., two spoons of ice cream. At five thirty, I had some chips and dip; at six forty-five, half a container of yogurt; at nine fifteen, some rice and one cup of buttermilk. At ten thirty, I had half a container of yogurt, and finally, at 11:40 p.m., I had two spoons of ice cream and one banana.

As I went to bed, we were extremely happy that it was a rare day when I did not thrown up.

23 Throwing Up – the Mystery Continues

I had gone to bed happy on November 27. The fact that I had not thrown up the whole day was creating a sense of hope. Dad thought his latest strategy of eating yogurt, buttermilk, and bananas was a great success. As we were going to bed, he even suggested that soon we might be able to go back to one millimeter per day for the next twenty-five days. In that case, we could steal one more inch out of this desperate situation.

Sunday morning, I woke up at seven thirty, took two pain medications, and then went back to sleep. We all got up at ten. Mom started cleaning the infected pin. She said, "It does not look all that bad." In retrospect, we believed that it was the tremendous amount of flexing Alex was doing that was causing the pins to move a lot inside the bone. This in turn was causing my body to excrete that white fluid. It probably wasn't an infection.

I did not throw up all day the previous day, and it seemed like I was on the road to recovery with Dad's yogurt therapy. I had exactly the same breakfast, at the same time, as the previous day. Why fool with the recipe for success?

My high school buddy Johnny Nastus came by to see me at noon. John had been the captain of the cross-country team last year. We were both on the team since our freshmen year. We had also wrestled to-gether on the same team since our sophomore year. John was very supportive ever since I began considering this surgery. A week before my surgery, John called me and gave me words of encouragement. He said he would come and see me frequently while I was recovering. He was keeping his word. Dad escorted John into my room, and then left us alone. We talked about this and that. He told me about his first year in college. For me, this surgery was pushing me one year back, and I was spending this time in my bed with two metal rings around my legs.

I asked John, "Are college girls prettier than the ones in our high school?"

"Yeah, man. Not only are they prettier, but they're smarter," he said.

"Oh, that's too bad." I was cracking jokes, but the smile from my face was fading. There was a sense of uneasiness in my stomach. Sud-denly, in mid-sentence, I stopped and said to John, "Can you call my dad real quick?"

John stepped out of the room. "Mr. Shukla, Akash is looking for you."

As soon as Dad heard that, he figured out what was happening. He came running to my room. I motioned towards the pink vomit tray. He picked it up, held it near my chest, and told John to wait in the kitchen. I started throwing up helplessly. The theory about yogurt therapy was out the window. The euphoria of last night, about stealing one more inch out of this situation, had evaporated.

We did not have the luxury of self-pity, no time to lick my wounds. I took one more pain medication, and had three spoons of ice cream. I threw myself from my bed to the wheelchair, from the wheel-chair to the car seat, and I was on my way to JCPT for my next therapy session. Alex was going to open the place just for me. The vomit epi-sode had delayed our departure from home and we were nervous that we would be late and keep Alex waiting.

On that Sunday there was no traffic on 287. As we took the exit for Route 27, I said, "We're going to be on time after all."

At the traffic light, two blocks before JCPT, there were many police cars. They had closed off the part of Route 27 that would take us to JCPT. I got very nervous. It wasn't just missing the appointment that I was worried about. The next day, we had to see Dr. Rozbruch. I needed to exercise my joints to their limit so when Rozbruch checked them, he could see a good range of motion. Only then would he allow us to continue lengthening. The police cars were not just blocking Route 27; they were blocking the further extension of my height.

There wasn't a single car on Route 27 coming or going beyond the barricade. We were forced to turn left on a crossroad, heading to the Costco Warehouse. We made a U-turn, and once again came out at the junction of Route 27. There was a police car three cars ahead of us, right in the middle of the intersection. Mom said, "Let me go explain to the cop that we have a medical emergency." She put the car in park and started walking towards the police car.

It turned out that there was a major power failure on the next four blocks of Route 27. None of the traffic lights were working. Because of that, the police had barricaded both sides of that section. JCPT's building was right in the middle of that closed-off section.

When Mom went to the police car, the officer in the front seat was apparently dozing off. When Mom said, "Excuse me, officer," he got startled and jumped. Mom said, "My son has gone through a very serious surgery. The therapy building, five hundred feet from here, is going to open especially today to give him therapy. He has a hospital appointment tomorrow and this therapy has to be done today."

The officer asked, "Where is your car?"

Mom said, "Three cars back."

He said, "Okay, I will let you go. Pull over to the left lane, pass me, and make a left at the light."

Mom came back with a smile on her face, "I knew he would let us through," she said. She got in the driver's seat, put the car in drive, and did what the officer had told her to do. As we passed the officer and turned left onto Route 27, the officer turned on his flashers and sirens, and came after us. Mom stopped the car.

The officer got out of his car and walked towards us. As Mom lowered her window, he said in a stern voice, "Where do you think you're going?"

Mom said, "You told me I could go."

He said, "Oh. I didn't know that was you." Obviously not one of New Jersey's finest- nor brightest!

We got to JCPT in two minutes. Alex wasn't there yet. We weren't sure whether the police would let him through the roadblock. It was already 1:35. The appointment was for one thirty. We waited for ten more minutes, and then Dad got his cell phone out. Just then, a green minivan pulled into the driveway and Alex stepped out. He had a brown bag in his hand.

Mom and Dad wheeled me to the door, and Alex unlocked it. He turned on the heating system and the stereo system. Before I started heading towards the low mat, he reached into the brown bag and took out a bottle of blueberry juice. He said, "My wife has sent this for Akash. It will settle the acid in his stomach." He then pulled out a bottle of buttermilk. He said, "And also this. The culture in buttermilk and yogurt replaces the good bacteria in the colon." Alex wasn't done yet. He got out a pumpkin bread, and said, "Caroline baked this specially for you."

I was very touched by this family's generosity. I was also happy that I was being treated by someone who cared for me in such a personal way.

Alex had me slide to the edge of the mat and dangle my feet over the edge. He then pushed my thighs down hard, ensuring that my feet were firm on the ground. I would reach out, grab his hands, and use them to pull myself up. Standing up did not come easily. I wanted to sit down in the worst way. After thirty seconds, I asked Alex, "How about sitting down?"

He said, "How about *no*." The negotiation would go on for another minute and a half. When Alex started flexing my ankle, I would be in so much pain I needed to hold my mom or dad's hands. As Alex would push

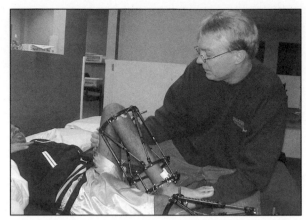

tighter, I would squeeze harder. On that particular day, Dad was taking a lot of pictures. The pictures were very telling and clearly showed the extent of the vigorous workout I was going through. We wanted to share them with Dr. Rozbruch the next day. Dad had always believed that a picture was worth a thousand words. We had to convince Dr. Rozbruch that we had the best physical therapists helping us so Dr. Rozbruch

would allow us to continue lengthening. Everything in life is marketing. Just because you're right, doesn't mean other people will know you're right.

That day, Alex worked on me for a total of one and a

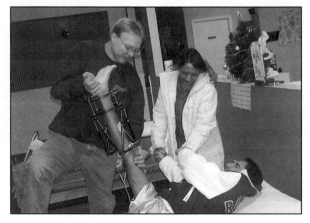

half hours. The ankle on which I could not put any weight only the previous day was now moving much more smoothly. This was nothing short of a miracle.

We got back home at four. As good as my ankle felt, the pain and exhaustion of the therapy had given me a splitting headache. I went to sleep and got up at six. During this time, Mom and Dad had started reviewing my activities for the last twenty days. Dad tried to create a mathematical correlation between vomit versus pain medication, vomit versus the type of food I ate, and vomit versus the time of the day. Once again, he could not see any correlation. He was very frustrated. Our puzzle seemed to have no solution.

Dad sat down and wrote all the facts as if he was writing a scientific report. He sat Mom and me down and said, "Maybe the most significant conclusion is that there is no correlation. What hypothesis can we derive from that conclusion? What if you throw up because of the sheer pain and the thought of it? Then there might not be any pattern."

So that was Dad's latest hypothesis- that the vomit was caused by pain and the fear of pain. That would explain why all the tests were coming normal, why my diet did not have an impact, and why changing from Vicodin to Darvoset to Hydromorphine did not make a difference. It was a plausible hypothesis, but so were so many of his previous theories.

Dad wrote a long e-mail and asked me if he should send such a long letter to Dr. Wagner. I said, "Yes. He is a good guy. I'm sure he will read every word." Mom said the same thing. Dad wasn't sure. Would Dr. Wagner think we were delving into something that was his area of expertise? Dr. Wagner seemed to be a genuinely compassionate, inquisitive doctor. We put our faith in our observation, and Dad e-mailed the letter at 7:24 p.m., on November 28.

From: Shukla Meena & Rahul

Sent: Sunday, November 28, 2004 7:24 PM

To: 'Wagner, Philip MD'

Subject: Akash vomit: November 28

Hello Dr. Wagner,

Thanks for your response to our e-mail last week. Even though you were on vacation, you took time to write and gave us many suggestions. We appreciate your help and your kind sympathetic words. Here I am with a long letter and I ask you to give your time to read it. Thank you for your time. We are facing a complicated puzzle. Only with your help can we hope to solve it. Here is what is happening:

Akash's Pain: His pain has been on the rise. Last two days, a pin seemed infected and causing more than usual pain. The infection is coming under control. His stomach has not settled down. It looks better for a day and then it acts up again.

Test Results: Akash's second blood test had a WBC of 11.7 (down from 17). All other items on the blood test were also normal or close to normal. The lab has not sent the results of his stool test but verbally told Akash's doctor that the results seem okay. His ultra sound showed nothing alarming.

Vomit does not go away: Akash's vomit started November 10. Today is November 28. In the eighteen days, he had six days without a vomit, ten days of one vomit per day and two days of two vomits per day. Just in the last five days, he vomited once on Wednesday, Thursday once, Friday twice, and Saturday, he did not throw up at all. Sunday (this morning), he threw up at eleven thirty a.m., an hour after breakfast. It is six p.m. and he has retained some very light food since his vomit.

Can't see a correlation: In my graduate studies, I studied Design of Experiments/Statistics and later did a lot of engineering research. Last few days, I have taken detailed notes of every single activity of Akash. I am so puzzled that I see no correlation between known factors and vomit. For instance, he took same medication, ate the same food, same quantity, at the same time of the day yesterday as he did today (exactly the same). Yesterday he did not vomit but today he did.

Medication History: From September 27 until November 10, when he first started vomiting, he was on Vicodin. Vicodin was changed to Darvoset on November 14. His vomit did not stop. Darvoset was replaced by Hydromorphine. He did not vomit for three days and then intermittent vomit started. During Thanksgiving, we had him off any pain medication for two days. He still had a vomit on the third day. On that day, we switched back to Vicodin, and he had a second vomit. Since the last three days, we gave him two Hydromorphine every three hours. It seemed like things were getting better, but he vomited today. From the start of his vomit (November 10) he has been taking Prochlorperzine, then Metoclopramide, and currently Trimethobenz (three times a day). There was not a day when Akash missed any of the doses for anti-nausea medicine. This is a giant puzzle.

Dr. Rozbruch told me that on pain management, you are one of the best he has ever known. I hope you can help us solve this puzzle. My son's physical therapy is going very well. If his pain and vomit would go away, he could regain the resolve to meet his height goals.

I was wondering:

Do you think just the pain could cause Akash to throw up at random times? That may explain why the same food and same medication cause vomit some days and not on other days.

Do you think a month and a half of Vicodin changes blood chemistry in such a way that his stomach would reject food at random times?

From September 24 to November 10 (the first day of the vomit), he had been on antibiotics for twenty-four out of forty-six days. Could that have destroyed good bacteria in his intestine and created toxins that are now causing this problem at random times?

Or do you think this may still be related to some unexplained GI problems and not to his pain or medication?

We are coming to see Dr. Rozbruch tomorrow afternoon. Is it possible to see you- even for a few minutes? If you can, please contact us at any of the following numbers.

Thank you very much, Doctor Wagner.

-Rahul

Once we sent the letter, we sat down to eat. I was very hungry. I had spaghetti with marinara sauce. I ate a little more than usual. We then started watching episodes of *LA Law*. Dad had theorized that my vomits occurred within ninety minutes of a meal. He kept staring at the clock. He was holding his breath, waiting for nine p.m. to pass. At eight thirty, Mom said, "Let's do pin care." Dad took her out and told her quietly to wait until ten. He said that the pain of pin care might unsettle the food in my stomach.

Mom started doing the pin care at ten and finished at eleven. Mom and Dad then sat down to eat. By the time we were ready to go to bed, it was twelve thirty a.m. The day hadn't ended yet. Dad quickly downloaded the pictures of this afternoon's therapy from the camera onto the computer. For the next half hour, he printed the pictures. We needed them for the next day.

The next day, we had to see Dr. Rozbruch. He was going to check my ankle motion, and then render his verdict. He could say, "That is it. No more!" Then this project would come to an end. We had also asked Dr. Wagner in the e-mail if we could see him while we were in New York. Dr. Wagner was a very busy doctor and it wasn't likely that at a moment's notice, he could give us an appointment.

We turned off the light at one thirty and went to sleep, wondering what was in store for us tomorrow.

24 Would the Doctor Let Me Go Up to 50 Millimeters (2 inches)?

Monday morning we kept checking the computer to see if there was a response from Dr. Wagner, but how could there be? We had sent the e-mail only the previous night. I did not think we would hear from him that day. Dad had to see his heart doctor in the morning and left at eight thirty. Mom started helping me get ready for my morning therapy appointment. We were leaving no stones unturned. It was Mom's idea to have one more therapy session just before our visit to Dr. Rozbruch. Sometimes, my joints seemed to freeze up really badly when I first woke up. Mom was worried that if we went to see Dr. Rozbruch in that condition, he might not fully recognize the extent of the improvement. She said, "Let Alex relax the joints and tissues, so Rozbruch can see the complete range of motion that you have achieved."

Once Dad came back, the three of us left for JCPT. We reached there at eleven. Alex started working on me. Later, Alex's wife, Caroline, came and stood next to me for a while. It was clear how everybody was rooting for me. Alex and Caroline had clearly taken this as a personal challenge.

That day, Alex brought a tape recorder with him. He told me that he was conducting a study for his doctorate program. He had to present a paper on the correlation of peoples' screams and the amount of pain that they were in. He thought I'd be an ideal candidate for this study. He turned on the tape recorder and started recording my screams. I was enjoying the diversion. When I wasn't screaming in pain, I started singing into the tape recorder. As he later told me, when Alex played the tape for his class, people could not believe the amount of pain someone had to sustain to go through this procedure.

As we were leaving, Alex said, "Let us know the minute you find out what the doctor says." They knew that today was the day of verdict. There was so much suspense and drama- not just for me but for my mom and dad also. They had invested every ounce of their emotional energy and every moment of their life into this project. What if Dr. Rozbruch said, "I can't let you go on?" In this litigious world, he might be more concerned about preventing a future lawsuit from a patient than to do the right thing. If he said, "Stop now," we would not have any other options available. This wasn't like getting your basement finished. If the contractor you were working with did not want to put the circular staircase in place of the regular staircase, you could fire that contractor and hire the one who would do what you want. If the doctor said no, we would have to accept it. Even if we thought he was wrong, we would not have the courage to disregard his advice and do something against his judgment.

Once we got out of the Holland Tunnel, Dad looked at his phone and said, "I have a missed call. Who," he wondered, "would call me on this phone?"

"Why?" I asked.

"I got this phone only two days ago, and have not given the number out to anybody." It was a new Blackberry 7100. It was their top-of-the-line phone, with PC synchronization, e-mail, and web surfing. Dad got the same fancy phone for me also. He thought making all the features work on this gadget would take my mind off the pain. As a matter of fact, I was looking at the various new features of my own new phone as we were driving to New York.

Dad looked at the number on the caller ID. It was the general number from the Hospital for Special Surgery. He said, "I had included this phone number in my e-mail to Dr. Wagner last night. Do you think he tried to call us on the cell phone?" We all thought it wasn't likely.

This was one of the very few appointments where Dr. Rozbruch did not want to get an x-ray done. He was only going to look at my ankle motion and tell us whether we could continue. We entered his office and let the receptionist know we were there. Omaira reminded Dad of the balance of $6,000 for the first surgery. We had already paid $12,000 on September 21. Dad gave her the Amex card and asked her to charge $6,000 on his card. The airline miles were piling up! Just then, the receptionist said, "Mr. Shukla, it is Dr. Wagner on the line. He has been trying to locate you for a while." As Mom was wheeling me into the examination room, Dad took Dr. Wagner's call.

"Hi. This is Dr. Wagner," he told Dad, "I'm going to be in surgery all day. As a matter of fact, I'm in the OR right now, but I got your e-mail and I wanted to discuss it with you."

"I'm so sorry for writing such a long e-mail," said Dad.

"No, no. That was quite all right. I read it all," replied Dr. Wagner. He then said, "You have an interesting hypothesis and I think you may be right. This *might* be purely pain related." He then said, "This is similar to what some of the chemotherapy patients go through. After a few chemotherapy sessions, on the day of chemotherapy, some patients start throwing up before chemotherapy starts because their bodies are so afraid of what is *going* to happen."

He discussed various options with Dad for the next fifteen minutes. Dr. Wagner wanted to take a completely different approach to my vomit situation. He said he was going to prescribe Zofran, a medication normally given to chemotherapy patients. He also wanted to give a special anti-nausea skin patch to be applied behind the ear. He said it was a half-inch diameter, medicated, sticky patch. He wanted us to cut it in half, because otherwise it might put too much medication in my system. Dr. Wagner took great pain in explaining how to cut the patch and how it should be applied. He said that he would be in the OR for the rest of the day but that he would make sure the prescription would be ready at his office, which was only minutes from Dr. Rozbruch's office. Dad thanked him, hung up, and came to the examination room.

He told Mom and me about his conversation with Dr. Wagner. We were deeply touched by the concern he showed. He knew from Dad's e-mail that we were going to be seeing Dr. Rozbruch that morning. When he could not contact us on our cell phone, he tracked us down in Dr. Rozbruch's office, all of this while he was in the operating room. I was right when I said on Thanksgiving Day we had many things to be thankful for. One of them was Dr. Wagner.

We were waiting for Dr. Rozbruch. Dr. Fragomen came in first. He always treated my family with a lot of respect. "Hello, Akash," he greeted me, and then turned to Mom and Dad and shook hands. He started pushing my ankle to see how close to neutral he could get it. We were staring at him, wondering what he would say. He had a smile on his face. As he started stepping out of the office, he turned his head and said, "Akash, Dr. Rozbruch will be pleased with what he will see."

Soon after, Dr. Rozbruch walked in with Dr. Fragomen. Dr. Rozbruch said, "Let's first look at the pin." He looked at the pin we thought was infected. He said, "It looks a lot better than in the picture." Maybe it was not infected after all. He then looked up at Dr. Fragomen and said, "Remember that patient we had last year? She had an infection from start to finish."

Dr. Fragomen nodded, and said, "She used to get sick much worse than Akash." Now he tells me, I thought to myself.

Mom pointed Dr. Rozbruch's attention to the pin at the immediate left of the pin they were discussing. She said, "Akash has been complaining about that pin also."

Rozbruch looked at that pin and then said, "This also seems infected, but does not look as bad as the other one. I'll have Arkady take a culture once I'm done."

He then turned his attention to checking my ankle motion. He pushed the left ankle gently and then the right ankle. Somehow, my ankles did not move as readily as they did at JCPT. I looked at Mom and Dad. They also looked disappointed and scared. Then Dr. Rozbruch pushed my right ankle with much more force. My ankle flexed much more than it did the last time I was in his office. As he was holding my ankle, Dr. Rozbruch looked at me and said, "Almost in neutral position."

The left ankle was tough to move because of my pin pain. But even there, once Rozbruch pushed it with force, he looked pleasantly surprised. Mom handed him the report that Alex had prepared on me. Alex had taken measurements of ankle movement angles and knee movement angles. As Dr. Rozbruch saw this, his face began looking more cheery. All the while, Dad was telling him about how good Alex and his team were at JCPT. This was a team performance for Mom, Dad, and me. No sooner would Dad complete a sentence praising JCPT, then Mom would jump in and add on to what he said. The purpose was to convince Dr. Rozbruch that I was in good hands and that it was unlikely that any other limb lengthening patients would have gotten therapy with this frequency, intensity, and quality.

Dad was holding all the pictures in his hand and was waiting for the right moment to show them to Dr. Rozbruch. We never knew that managing this medical project would require such a high level of diplomacy. If we sold too hard, we would look like pushy patients. If we didn't explain clearly and if Dr. Rozbruch decided not to continue, it would be the biggest setback of my life.

Dad held the pictures in a way that Rozbruch would get a glance. He said to Dad, "What is that you have, pictures?"

That was the opening Dad was looking for. "I took some pictures to show you the intensity of the therapy that Akash is receiving." Dad put ten pictures in Rozbruch's hands.

As Rozbruch thumbed through them, one after another, he had an expression of surprise and admiration on his face. He said, "Wow, it looks like they know what they're doing." He then turned to me and said, "How much height do you have to get out of this so the emotional investment would be worth your while?"

I said, "I need to get at least two inches."

"That is achievable. But I don't think it's advisable to go beyond two inches."

There was a collective sigh of relief in the room. I silently said 'Thank you, Lord!'

The hell I had convinced myself to go through for the last ten days had paid off.

Dad said, "That is great. Two inches will make us happy." I looked at Mom. She had a look of relief on her face. Although only twenty days ago, we were dreaming of getting three-and-a-quarter inches out of this, the events of the last ten days had made us realize that two inches would be a huge success.

"You should continue at a half a millimeter per day," said Rozbruch.

Dad said, "What if, with what Alex is doing, we could speed things up and get it over with before December 24th?" The true motive for Dad saying what he said was quite different. He was indirectly asking if going beyond two inches was possible.

Rozbruch said, "For one thing, I do not have any dates available for surgery in December. So even if you achieve the remaining twelve millimeters in a shorter time, you would still have to wait until January. Secondly," he said, "Let us take things slowly."

Dad wanted to suggest that if things were going well after December 24, could we continue lengthening until the scheduled date of the second surgery? He didn't say any of that. Rozbruch had just okayed two inches. If we pushed for going over two inches prematurely, once he said no, it would be difficult to move him from that position. Rozbruch said, "Let me step out and see the availability of the date for the surgery to take these rings out." He came back in a few minutes and said, "It looks like January 5th or January 10th." We opted for the 5th.

Feeling playful at the time, I looked at him with fake sincerity on my face. "Dr. Rozbruch," I said in a concerned voice, "Once these rings are off, the entire procedure is finished, and I'm fully healed, will I be able to ski?"

He said, "I can't see any reason why not."

"That's strange," I said in a mischievous tone, "Because I couldn't ski before the surgery."

He stopped for a moment, shook his head, and burst into laughter. "Knowing you, I should have seen that coming," he said.

Light moments like this were few and far between. Overall, the pain and suffering had taken its toll on me, and it was slowly melting my resolve. Mom and Dad were encouraging me to get every last millimeter out of this project. But I had had enough. I wanted to get it over with. Just hearing a definite date when these rings would come off made me very happy.

Dr. Blyakher came in to take a quick culture of my infected pins with a cotton swab. Then we got ready to leave. Dr. Rozbruch and Dr. Fragomen's faces were beaming. Dr. Fragomen said, "We were all hoping that this would be a success for Akash, and now that it is happening, we are very happy."

As Mom wheeled me to the parking lot garage, Dad ran across the street to Dr. Wagner's office to pick up the prescription. Then we were on our familiar road from FDR to the Holland Tunnel. We were happy and excited. Dad told me how well he thought I handled myself. He said I was funny and pleasant. My face looked healthy and fresh.

Once we were out of the Holland Tunnel, Mom called Alex. Both Mom and Dad thanked him for the work he and Reena had done. As we entered the New Jersey Turnpike, I started having a headache. "Let's call Auntie and give her the good news."

Auntie had been with us for fifteen years, then she retired and left for India in 2001. She came to the USA for a visit in 2003. She came to stay with us for a short period. During that time, Dad had his heart attack. Auntie wasn't going to leave us at that time. Dad's health situation was unsettled for a whole year. If Sushi Auntie hadn't been with us at that time, it would have been very difficult. Once Dad was well, she was thinking about going back to India again. She was seventy-one at that time. Just at that time, we were making the final decisions on my surgery. I explained to her how they would cut my bone, put screws in my leg, and stretch the bone. When she heard about it, she started crying. There was no way she was going to leave us before my surgery. She thought she would leave for India right after my surgery.

After the surgery, when she saw the rings bolted to my legs, she gasped. She knew she would not be able to leave me until the rings came off. When Mom would do the daily pin care, Auntie would be holding my hand, or cutting strips of Xeroform tape. After I took my morning showers, she would help Mom dry all my pins with a hair dryer. Best of all, since Mom was always busy with me from morning until night, she always made sure that breakfast, lunch, and dinner were ready.

I called from the car and told Auntie, "Doctor Rozbruch has said we can continue lengthening. I will be able to reach two inches after all."

She was thrilled. She kept saying, "God has been looking after you."

By the time we got on Route 78 from the New Jersey Turnpike, my mild headache was turning into a splitting headache. By the time we got home, I could barely talk because of the headache. My eyes had turned glassy and red. The face that looked healthy and fresh in the morning looked very sickly in the afternoon.

I went to my bed. Dad sat next to me and started rubbing special oil in my head. Mom sat near my feet and started helping me do ankle exercises. I whispered, "We did it."

"No, *you* did it," Mom said.

25 Throwing Up – the Mystery Is Solved

The trip to New York had been tiring as usual. While I took a quick nap, Dad went to the pharmacy and purchased the new medication. I took one Zofran right away. Mom cut the patch in a half circle and placed it behind my right ear. I told Dad his theory finally seemed to have panned out. It was the pain all along. Now that we had zeroed in on the cause, it was possible to use the correct drug therapy. All three of us were sure the vomit problem was finally resolved.

But all of us were very tense all day the next day. We were losing our cool on small matters. One would think that the anxiety level in the Shukla family would have greatly reduced after our visit with Dr. Rozbruch. It wasn't so. The stress level in our family was reaching new heights. On the surface, I was thrilled that Dr. Rozbruch had okayed going up to two inches. But at some deeper level, I was deeply disappointed that he did not say, "Stop lengthening." Maybe then, he would have taken me to the operating room right away and the damn frames would have come off. Now I was looking at twenty more days of distraction, aches in my body, the daily torture of pin care, and God knows what else. I know now, but did not know at that time, that I had started losing my objectivity.

Mom was working with me from early morning until late night. What she did, several full-time nurses could not do. There was so much more stuff coming out from the pin wounds that pin care now took ninety minutes. It was also much more painful. She did it expertly; better than most medical professionals would do. My screams had become much louder and would fill the entire house. People sitting in other rooms would feel as if someone was in a torture chamber and screaming. Many times, visitors sitting in other rooms could not bear the sound of my screams. How Mom maintained her focus for more than an hour is beyond me.

But by now, I was mentally exhausted and near a nervous breakdown. That day, I said I did not think I needed ankle belt stretch exercises. She explained to me why now was not the time to give up. I said, "You don't know what I am going through."

Dad was focused on strategizing- how to stop my vomit, how to convince Rozbruch to continue lengthening, how to keep my frame of mind positive, how to renegotiate the hospital bill with the hospital administrator, and above all, how not to leave a fraction of a millimeter on the table.

I had a light lunch and several small snacks throughout the day. The new anti-nausea patch seemed to be working. I had taken the new pills, Zofran and Famotidine. By night, I was hungry- a good sign. Mom quickly made some penne pasta. I sat down to eat at ten thirty pm. Pasta tasted so good. I had a small second serving.

At midnight, I threw up.

Oh, yes. It happened ninety minutes after a meal. Dad had a long face. He looked lost. Once I finished throwing up, he asked me, "Why did you take a second serving?" His face was getting red. I did not say anything, just looked at him with a sad stare. He asked loudly "Why did you take a second serving? Can't you think?" It looked as if his veins were ready to pop. He said, "Did you chew your food correctly? Maybe you don't chew your food right." By now, he wasn't talking. He was screaming.

Mom walked to him and said, "Calm down. You thought with new medication, you had solved the problem. Now with his vomit, you feel that you are not in control. You're taking your frustration out on Akash."

Dad stopped screaming. He looked broken and he rushed out of the room. He came back five minutes later and said to Mom, "You are right. I feel so helpless." He turned to me and said, "I'm sorry. This wasn't your fault." We knew this surgery was pushing everyone to a breaking point.

On Tuesday, November 30, I did not throw up for the whole day. Then all day Wednesday, I did not throw up. The new medication seemed to have been working after all. That should have calmed us down, but it had an opposite effect. If I did not throw up for two days in a row, and then threw up, that would be a bigger setback then if I was throwing up every day. Everyone in the house was tense. If I said I was feeling nauseous, Mom, Dad, and Sushi Auntie looked frightened.

On Thursday, December 2, we were all sitting at the breakfast table and talking about the vomit-free two days. Dad said, "Make sure you take pain medication every four hours, whether or not you're in pain." He was still clinging to his hypothesis that it was the pain that was causing the vomit and not the medication.

Mom said, "Maybe he should take it if he feels extreme pain."

"You just don't understand. When we have a theory, we have to stick to it," Dad said.

"No, you don't understand," said Mom.

What started as a simple discussion soon turned into a huge argument. I had to calm them both. I had read that fear makes you lose your objectivity. That was happening to my family. I had two consecutive vomit-free days. As a result, we were even more nervous. One false step and I would start vomiting. If I didn't vomit, I could exercise better. If I could exercise, maybe we could go beyond two inches.

Friday, December 3, I had gone through four days of no vomit. The therapy at JCPT was going well. We were racking up the bills. I was still doing two sessions a day. The ankle motion was the best it had been. Mom, Dad, and I discussed the possibility of making four adjustments a day instead of three. We weren't sure if Rozbruch would go along with that. Dad had theorized that Dr. Rozbruch's mind was already made up and that Dr. Rozbruch wanted us to stop lengthening. Dad said when we saw Dr. Rozbruch on November 22- the day when he said to stop length-ening- Dr. Rozbruch had found out about my stiff ankle motion and the burning toes only halfway through his examination.

"But, " Dad said, "he told us about the date for the frame removal as soon as he came in the room. That would mean, he is not comfort-able with continuing the lengthening."

I went into this surgery thinking that if I did all the right things, I would be able to push it to three inches. I wanted the rings (the "fuck-ing rings," by now) to come out as soon as possible. But I would not mind getting faster lengthening in the meantime. Dad made four ad-justments on December 3 just to see how I could handle it. All was well. He then wrote a nice e-mail to Dr. Rozbruch, explaining how well everything was- no vomit, ankle motion was excellent, no burn-ing of toes, and pins looked clean. He then indirectly suggested that going from three adjustments to four might be a good idea. We were sure Dr. Rozbruch would give his blessings.

Dr. Rozbruch didn't go along with the idea. Even though the e-mail did not specifically ask whether we should change to four struts per day, he read in-between the lines, and sent us a one-line response: "Do not speed up the rate of distraction." So much for that plan. We went back to three adjustments per day immediately.

Since I had not had a vomit in four days, my energy level had im-proved considerably. Going to JCPT was becoming somewhat more enjoyable. I saw Reena every day. She always had a charming smile and a professional determination. She had the correct blend of humor and military-like authority.

At JCPT, the first thing I would do was sign my name on a card. Whereas other patients would stay on the same card for months, in my case, they had to staple several cards in only two weeks. Other patients would not exceed the number of therapies approved by the insurance company. Since my coverage was declined, I was not restricted by the insurance company.

Once I signed in, I would wheel myself to the other end of the hall. There, I would get out of the chair, and transfer onto the mat. Reena would ask me to lie on my stomach, which I always found to be very difficult. She would then put pillows under my thighs to decrease the pain. Next, she would bend my knee as much as she could, and then measure the angle.

In another exercise, Reena would stand in front of me. One of her aides would stand to my right. The aide would hold a stack of eleven cups in his hand. I had to stretch my arms and legs, reach the topmost cup in the aide's right hand, and then place it on her left hand. Reena explained to me, "When you stretch, it forces your body weight on your heels."

In one of the most painful exercises, Reena would stand on the middle of the table, making sure to plant her feet. She would then lift my leg into the air, and put *all* of her weight on it. She would push my toes upward and stretch my ankles. She would hold this for a count of forty. To make it more interesting, and to involve me in it, she would say one number and ask me to say the next number. Though this didn't 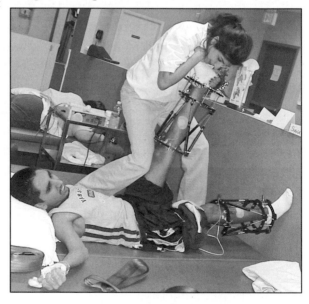 make it any less painful, it helped put my mind somewhere else.

There were many other routines where I used many exercise machines. One of the last exercises was the most tiring one. With my walker, I would walk about fifty steps. During this time, Reena, with her hands on my shoulders, trying to make sure I was standing straight, would give me instructions. Justin would walk behind me with a wheelchair. They would get me near the reception desk where Mom or Dad would be waiting for me.

Every time I talked to Dr. Rozbruch about my therapy with Reena, I would refer to her as "the pretty therapist." However, I used to tell Reena and Alex, "If you break the word therapist into two words, it becomes *the rapist*!"

My half an hour sessions routinely lasted for ninety minutes. I was doing two such sessions a day. Before the surgery, Dr. Rozbruch had suggested that it might be a good idea to work with professional therapists in half an hour sessions, 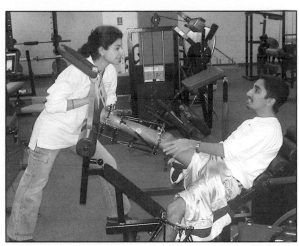 twice a week. Instead of that suggested rate of one hour per week, I was doing eighteen hours per week.

On December 3, I got back from my session at eleven thirty. I had two slices of apple and a donut. A little later, I had bread, vegetables, pudding, and yogurt. By two forty-five, Mom was loading me back in the car and driving me back to JCPT. My life had become a continuous string of therapy.

As we were exiting Route 287, I looked helplessly at Mom, reached for the vomit tray, and threw up. The "ninety-minute rule" still applied. I then called Dad. He was in a meeting. I told his assistant, Mrs. Dhingra, "Tell Dad I threw up."

She knew I had four vomit-free days. What was happening with my health was being followed closely by many people at Dad's company. Mrs. Dhingra sounded disappointed. She said, "I am so sorry to hear that Akash. I'll tell your Dad as soon as he gets out." Later, when Dad got out of the meeting and was going back to his office, Mrs.

Dhingra stopped him outside and said, "Akash called." She had a sad and worried look on her face. Dad knew that something had gone wrong. She said, "Akash had a vomit."

"Oh no," said Dad. He went into his office, locked his door, and collapsed in his chair. "This can't start all over again," he said to himself. Plus, if the latest theory was wrong, what other theory would he cling on to?

He did not know that I had called from the car, so he called home. Auntie answered the phone. Dad said, "I heard that Akash threw up."

Auntie knew nothing about it. She said, "Akash was complaining about being nauseous when he left."

Then my cell phone rang. We were just entering JCPT. "How are you doing, Son?" Dad asked.

I said, "Dad, it was a big one. It lasted for more than two minutes. Everything came out."

Dad said, "Can you still go through with therapy?"

I once again used my Gandhi-like accent and said, "I have got to do what I have got to do." We both laughed a nervous, phony laugh.

The second therapy of the day was a tough one. The vomit had drained all my energy and I was already tired from that morning's vigorous session. I reached home at five forty-five. Mom prepared some chips and onion dip for me. Dad got home at six thirty. I was in my room and Mom was taking a shower. Dad came to my room. I looked at him with a blank stare on my face, "Dad, what are we going to do now?" I was frightened that the streak of vomit would come back, and I would be right back where I was.

"I don't know, Son," said Dad. He had a rare defeated look on his face, "But we have only twenty more days to go. Somehow, we will survive this. So what if we have a vomit every day or two? We won't let that stop us or slow us down."

I had a light meal at seven forty-five. Then we waited. If I cleared the ninety-minute period, then I would not have a vomit. For the next ninety minutes, I needed to take my mind off the thought of vomit. We started watching a movie, *Twisted*. The movie was a bit gory. I didn't think that would help calm my stomach. We switched to watching the old reruns of *LA Law*. It had mystery, intrigue, and humor- but no blood. We watched three episodes of *LA Law* back-to-back. I looked at the wall clock. It was ten thirty. I said "Thank you, God, and thank you, *LA Law*."

The next day began with taking Zofran and Famotidine (anti-nausea) at eight thirty. An hour later, I took antibiotics; forty-five minutes later, Hydromorphine for pain; and four hours later, one more Hydromorphine. One hour later, I took a second antibiotic; two hours later, I took Zofran; forty-five minutes later, calcium; fifteen minutes later, Hydromorphine; three hours later, Famotidine; and half an hour later, Hydromorphine. Another half an hour later, I took two Colace (for easy bowel movement); one Singulair (for seasonal allergies); and one Hydroxezine (which prevented a rash that tended to break out on me). The day wasn't done yet. At 11:50 at night, I took antibiotics, Zofran, and a calcium tablet. An hour later, at 12:50, a last Hydromorphine, and then I went to sleep.

The above fun-filled schedule wouldn't be complete without frequent small snacks. I needed to keep my energy up and get enough nutrients so the bone growth would be satisfactory. I would have milk, yogurt, potato chips, bread, salad, and broccoli at properly spaced intervals. Before the surgery, I jokingly used to say, "I am trying to gain more height so that I can date taller babes." Looking at the above list of daily intake, I thought to myself, "I don't mind the screws and bolts sticking into my flesh or the excruciating therapy. But yogurt and broccoli . . . you've got to be kidding me!"

On that day, along with this hectic schedule, I had two therapy sessions, one hour of pin care, and several at-home exercise routines. The next day, Alex opened JCPT especially for us.

Dr. Wagner had changed directions for pain and nausea medication on November 28. Since then, I threw up twice: once on November

28 and once again, four days later, on Friday, December 3, on my way to therapy. I did not throw up Saturday and Sunday.

And as I would later find out, the vomit on December 3 would be my last vomit. The mystery was finally solved and the darkest days of this limb-lengthening project were finally behind me!

26 Can We Get a Little More Than 2 Inches

Now that this major crisis was behind us, we were able to attend to other matters, such as the expenses for the surgery. Back in August, Omaira had given us an estimate for the total cost around $150,000. That by itself was a huge amount. Dr. Rozbruch's fee for the first phase was going to be $20,000 and the hospital cost was expected to be $60,000. The insurance company had already told us that they would not pay a penny. When we first went to the hospital, we had made an advance payment of $30,000. Then before I was discharged, they put another $35,000 on Dad's charge card.

We thought we were done paying for the hospital stay. Once we came home from the first surgery, we started receiving bills from the hospital. They would not send us an itemized bill. It would be a one-page statement, with one line on it. All it would state was that the total cost for six days in the hospital was $93,000. We were not happy about this, but how much could we fight it? I still had to go to the hospital in January for the next phase of the surgery. In that phase, the doctor would drill a hole right below my kneecap into the tibia. He would then insert an IM (intramedullary) rod into the center cavity of the bone. The rod had to go through the gap created by the distraction. The doctor would then secure the bone to the rod with five screws- two below my knee, two above my ankle, and one in the lower ankle.

The screws would not protrude through the skin. The screws on the IM rod would keep the extended bone in position. Only then would the doctor remove the external rings.

If the first surgery went 50 percent over their estimate, we were afraid what would happen with the second surgery. Dad had a plan. He said, "We will go see the case manager personally. Some things you do over the phone; some things you do face to face." He also wanted to make sure I went along with him, sat there in my wheelchair, and created additional dramatic effect.

I said, "Let us take the notes for my book and tell them about it." In the meantime, Dad thought we should also seek help from Dr. Rozbruch on settling the bill with the hospital. He wrote a letter to Dr. Rozbruch on December 5.

```
Hello Dr. Rozbruch,

Thanks for your prompt response. We are pro-
ceeding the distraction at the unchanged rate of
half a millimeter per day. Akash is doing okay.
The suspect pin still shows occasional discharge,
especially after the therapy. Meena thinks that
it might be the result of a lot of workout. The
JCPT therapists do ninety-minute sessions twelve
times a week. That is 1,000 minutes of therapy
per week and may be putting a lot of pressure on
the pins. We still wonder, whether the antibiot-
ics have successfully arrested the infection.
Before we stop the antibiotics, it might be a
good idea to come visit you, perhaps early this
week. If you can fit us in, we do not mind the
costs of additional visits. All else is going so
well and we do not want to take any more chances.
We would feel a lot better if you'd look at this.
His last x-rays were on November 22- three weeks
ago. It may be a good idea to get that out of the
way too.
```

The main reason for this letter, is to bring up certain financial matters so that I can settle them next time we come to see you.

Pre-Payment of 2005 fees: When we bring our payments up-to-date with Omaira this week, we would prefer to prepay your fees for the procedures that are still pending. If you could estimate your fees for surgeries as well as the future office visits, we would like to pay all of it now. As you know, the insurance company is not covering any of these expenses. Our only relief may come from taking a possible deduction on my tax return. Since medical expenses are allowed only over 7.5 percent of the gross income, I will need to combine all my medical expenses. We would appreciate it if there were any discounts or breaks for making the payments in advance. But if not, we would still appreciate it if you could work with us on this and let us combine all our payments now. Of course, we completely understand that on medical matters, no one can predict the costs, due to unforeseen circumstances. For that reason, if you later need to make adjustments to your estimates, we will completely understand.

Can we get your assistance with Hospital fees: The bill for the first phase from HSS has been very high ($93,000). This is quite a bit higher than their own initial estimates. We are somewhat fearful that they are charging us way more money than they would an insurance company. We do not have any bargaining power when we deal with them. If you have any influence with them- and know their administrative staff- maybe you can put in a good word for us. Tell them we are nice people(maybe lacking in modesty). Tell them about the positive publicity HSS will get from Akash's book. *Newark Star Ledger* is thinking of doing an article on Akash sometime in January. The chief editor for **Machine Design** magazine has expressed interest in doing an article on Akash.

 I can say all those things to the hospital, but if they come from you, it will have much more impact. If your office can help us with this, we will be very grateful. All I am look-ing for is that they do not charge me more than their normal fees. I know I have no right to ask you for this favor, and if you would rather not, I will understand.

 All else is well. Hope you can see us this week.

    -Rahul

There were two reasons for asking Dr. Rozbruch to see us. Not only did we want him to look at my pins, but we were also hoping that he would let us continue beyond two inches. He sent an e-mail and told us to see him Tuesday, December 7.

Dad was calling the Accounts Receivable people at the hospital to negotiate a more reasonable amount for their bill. He talked to Yolanda and then to Jennifer at Accounts Receivable. They were sym-pathetic to our arguments but said that there was not much they could do. Dad said to me, "Somehow we will have to convince them to be-come more reasonable."

December 6 was a busy day for me. Dad and I reviewed the mov-ies he had taken of my therapy. We selected the clips we wanted to include in a short, five-minute DVD. We wanted to take that DVD with us the next day and show it to Dr. Rozbruch. The improvement in my ankle motion was phenomenal. The therapy I was receiving was so unbelievably extraordinary that unless we showed actual movies, nobody would believe the extent, the intensity, and the quality of it. Getting the movie from the tape to the DVD was a long process. Once the DVD was prepared, we would take a laptop with us. We would have to find the right moment during my conversation with Dr. Rozbruch somehow to bring up this movie. He was a busy man and might not want to spend time to see the movie. My entire family would have to practice a lot of diplomacy.

We were also going to do a show-and-tell for Jennifer of Accounts Receivable at HSS. Dad made photocopies of my book notes and his book notes and put them in a thick three-ring binder. Under the plastic cover of the binder, I put a page of the intended title: *How I Increased My Adult Height By Two Inches- A Painful Success Story in Limblengthening Surgery*.

On December 7, we were scheduled to see Dr. Rozbruch at two p.m. As usual, Mom made an appointment for a vigorous therapy session just prior to my appointment with Rozbruch. We finished the therapy at JCPT at eleven and were on our way to New York. On this particular day, we had a lot of extra things to carry. We had a laptop, a thick three-ring binder, reading material, a water bottle, medication, and of course, our digital camera. We never went anywhere without a camera.

Once in Dr. Rozbruch's office, Mom, Dad, and I were quickly taken to the examination room. Dr. Rozbruch came in and started looking at my ankle motion. Although I had not explicitly asked in the last twenty days whether he would allow us to go over fifty millimeters, he knew what was on my mind. He moved my ankle back and forth. It was coming almost to a neutral position. This was nothing short of a miracle. Only twenty days ago, I could barely bring it to "lacking fifteen degrees." He looked happy and said, "This looks very good."

Then there was a long pause.

He then said, "The next question you're going to ask me is whether we can keep going." He put his hand on his chin and thought about it for a while. He said, "Everything in life is a risk. We just have to make sure it is manageable."

Dad jumped in, saying, "I had a long discussion with a bank attorney once. I told her, 'You can never eliminate risk 100 percent. You just make it 'manageable'." Dad blurted all this in a hurry. He was not looking for a response. We just wanted Rozbruch to understand that eliminating a risk completely wouldn't be a wise strategy. This was a somewhat blatant effort in swaying his opinion. It was a risky strategy. What if he was offended with our wise-ass remarks and said no just to show who was the doctor in the room?

Rozbruch didn't say anything for a few seconds. I was getting nervous. Then, with a triumphant smile, he said, "I think Akash should get a few more millimeters out of this." We all breathed sighs of relief. We finally got what we wanted.

Dr. Rozbruch said, "Arkady, can you prepare a new chart?"

Dr. Blyakher turned to Dad and said, "Where are you at on the original distraction chart?"

The original chart had October 4 as day zero and went up to November 23 as day fifty. This was based on a rate of distraction of one millimeter per day. Of course, because of various setbacks, my rate of distraction had slowed down. On December 7, I had reached a distraction of forty-three millimeters and thus I was on day forty-three on the original chart. For instance, strut number one on the right leg had started at 202 on October 4. By December 7, it had advanced to a position of 241.

Dad gave his charts to Dr. Blyakher to look at. We were hoping that Dr. Rozbruch would okay at least ten more millimeters, which would take strut number one on the right leg up to 260. Instead, Dr. Rozbruch said to Dr. Blyakher, "Take a rate of .6 millimeters per day and see how far we can go by January 3."

Dad said, "You should make it 0.67 millimeters. That would require me to adjust four struts a day. 0.6 will not give me an easy-to-follow pattern."

Dr. Rozbruch said, "No, let's keep it at 0 .6 millimeters per day."

I don't think Dad liked that. To someone else, there's not much of a difference between .6 and .67. To Dad, we were leaving 0.07 millimeters on the table every day. He said to Rozbruch, "I think 0.6 millimeters a day will not give a user-friendly chart."

Rozbruch said in a determined tone, "No- leave it at 0.6 millimeters."

Dr. Blyakher went to his office, came back with two white sheets of paper, and gave them to Dad. The first strut would go up to 257 by January 3. I would get seven more millimeters than the original two inches. This was a miracle. Only twenty days ago, even one and a half inch seemed questionable. I could not believe my good fortune. Dr. Rozbruch saw the smile on my face and said, "Now Akash, keep exercising and don't get complacent."

"I won't," I said, "especially because I don't know what 'complacent' means."

Rozbruch broke out laughing. Everyone in the room was laughing hard. Rozbruch said, "Listen, you are a smart guy. I'm just a bone doctor." He then said, "An editor for the feature story with the *New York Times*- his name is Gardiner Harris- is doing an article and working with me. Can I give him your name? Would you  talk to him? He can protect your identity and not reveal your name if you don't want him to."

I said, "No, no- he can use my name and my picture. I don't mind."

As we were leaving Dr. Rozbruch's office, Mom went to see Omaira, Rozbruch's office manager. We wanted not only to pay any balance due on the surgery of September, but we wanted to prepay for the upcoming surgery for the ring removal and rod insertion. She put $21,300 dollars on her American Express charge card.

Once we got out of Dr. Rozbruch's office, we had to find Jennifer's office. The administration office of the hospital was only one building away. Once we were in the building, Mom, Dad, and I saw that there were no signs showing where the accounting office would be. I don't think customers or clients ever came to see anybody in accounting. Once Dad found out where Jennifer's office was, Dad started wheeling me down the narrow congested hallway. There were boxes full of paper in the hallway. It was quite a task to navigate the wheelchair to the office area. I could have just waited in the lobby, but Dad thought that this woman needed to see for herself what I went through. Only then would she feel a personal connection, which would make her more likely to offer a compromise.

Jennifer was a very pleasant and caring woman. As Mom, Dad, and I sat in front of her desk, Dad started telling her the entire story of what I had gone through. I then told what my motivations were, how difficult this surgery was, and how I was going to write a book about it.

"You're kidding." She looked at me admiringly. "You're writing a book?"

I said, "Yes, I want to share my experience with everyone."

Dad said, "If you insist on charging $93,000 for six days stay in the hospital, the whole world is going to find out about it. The future candidates for such a surgery will shy away from using your hospital. I had gotten estimates from Sinai Hospital in Baltimore. Their charges were a lot less. Why generate bad publicity? You should bring it up with your superiors. We are not looking for big concessions. We just want you to go back to your original estimates. I think you should charge a total of $100,000 for all three surgeries."

She nodded sympathetically and said, "Let me see what I can do. I will speak with Ross Sadler. He's the decision maker."

"Can we see him now?" I asked.

She said, "No, he's out. But I'll give you his phone number so you can call him."

As we left her office, we were hopeful that she would come through for us. We had a major surgery coming up on January 5. At that time, the rings would come out and an IM rod would be inserted in the tibia. A four-day hospital stay was estimated for that. Next, sometime in March, there would be a quick surgery to remove a couple of screws holding the IM nail into the tibia. That would be an ambulatory surgery. We were hoping to settle for $100,000 for all three surgeries. We also wanted to prepay those surgeries so that we could take it as medical expenses for the tax return of 2004.

There was one more thing we needed to do while in the hospital area. I had run out of my pain medication, Hydromorphine. Hydromorphine is a controlled substance. The pharmacy did not accept telephone refills nor did they accept photocopies of refills. The prescription had to be written on special paper. While Mom and I proceeded from Jennifer's office to the garage, Dad ran up to Dr. Wagner's office to pick up the prescription.

On our way home, I said to Dad, "We never got around to showing Dr. Rozbruch the movie of the therapy."

Dad said, "Everything in life is a delicate balance. If he thought we were selling too hard, he would think of us as a pushy family and might harden his position. As Bob Hope said," Dad used his favorite quotation, "Timing is everything."

Throughout the ride back home, Dad kept staring at the new distraction chart. "Something does not make sense here." He kept shaking his head. "The numbers don't seem right. If you move all six struts by one position, you should get one millimeter. To do 0.6, you would need to do between three to four struts every day. This new chart has all the struts going up by one tomorrow. That would mean that there would be days when none of them would go up."

By the time we got home, it was six p.m. and as usual, I had a giant headache. The trips to New York were always very tiring. Mom quickly did the pin care. My headache had gotten even worse.

At seven forty-five, we were on our way to JCPT for my second therapy session of the day. Now that the doctor had given me permission to go up to sixty millimeters, this was no time to let up on therapy.

27 Strategies, Negotiations and Pleas for a Few More Millimeters

A s Mom and I were on our way to JCPT for my second session of therapy for the day, Dad stayed home and started working on the charts of distraction. He entered the entire new chart in Excel, dividing six strut values for the left leg and six strut values for the right leg in 278 rows for the remaining twenty-eight days. Then for each strut position, he took the strut value for a day and deducted it from the value for the previous day. If the result was zero, it would indicate that that strut did not need to be moved up for that day. If that happened once in awhile, it would be okay. But if that happened frequently, it would not be good.

Excel did its calculations, and there were five days out of twenty-eight where not a single strut would require an adjustment. At the other extreme, there were eight days where all six struts required an adjustment. There were eight days where only two struts out of six would require adjustment. Overall, this would be a very uneven way of doing the distraction. The computer program by the manufacturer of the rings was probably prepared for only one millimeter distraction and did not work well when the distraction was slowed down to 0.6 millimeters per day.

Dad quickly wrote an e-mail to Dr. Rozbruch describing the un-even rate of distraction. Dad suggested that for the time being, we should continue using the schedule from the old chart and do four adjustments per day. Dad said that there was no rush on getting the numbers that got us beyond fifty millimeters, because we could use the numbers from the old chart for at least fifteen more days.

Dr. Rozbruch wrote back quickly. He was surprised with the erroneous numbers generated by the computer program (probably supplied by Smith & Nephew, the manufacturers of the Taylor Spatial Frame). He said, "This just goes to show how humans are smarter than computers." He gave us the okay to do four struts a day from the old chart. Dad got his 0.67 millimeters per day after all.

We knew that as long as Dr. Rozbruch's office prepared the chart for us, they had the ultimate control of how far we could go. If they didn't want us to go beyond a certain number, all they had to do was not give us the details of adjustments for the struts beyond that number. Not that we would ever do anything without the doctor's approval, but it would strategically help us if we somehow did not have to depend on getting this information from them. Dad, who was a lifelong student of statistics, sat down with me and explained to me the principles of regression analysis. He said, "When you have two variables, and you suspect a relationship between the two, treat one as a dependant variable and another as an independent variable. The relationship can be defined by a straight line equation $Y=mX+b$. In our case, "Y" would be the strut position for a given day number, "X" would be the day number, "m" would be the calculated slope of the relationship, and "b" as an intercept. Excel can compute all of that and the degree of confidence. If that comes out 80% or better, we can use the equation to calculate the strut value for any future day number."

The original strut adjustment chart started from day number one and ended at day number fifty. If we wanted to project the chart beyond day number 50, all we needed was to figure out the formula.

When we did the regression analysis in Excel, we came up with a degree of confidence of more than 99 percent for each strut position. Now that we had figured out the relationship, we could make our own chart. Table 1 in the Appendix shows the original distraction chart and

Table 2 in the Appendix shows the projected values beyond day number fifty.

On December 14, Dad sent an e-mail to Rozbruch, stating that we could extend the chart for eight more millimeters. Dad explained his logic, sent a newly constructed chart to Dr. Rozbruch for his review, and asked if we could start following this chart to go up to fifty-eight millimeters. Rozbruch said yes. There was a great sense of accomplishment in my entire family. We had successfully brought the target to fifty-eight millimeters.

The happiness of getting things this far did not dilute my pain. I was doing two therapies a day. My whole family had become very close to Reena and Alex. They would try to give me a slot where they could spend more time with me, like at the end of the day, so that they would not have an appointment after me. At night, often I was one of the last people leaving their building. Often the forty-five-minute session lasted for two hours. There was never an extra charge for that.

Although this was a wonderful thing and it was keeping my ankle motion where it needed to be, the sessions were getting much more painful. Reena used many different routines for the two hours of the therapy. In one, I would stand up, holding Reena's shoulders, and an aide (another pretty girl) would throw a blue playground ball about the size of a basketball at me. She would throw it such that I would have to stretch to the side in order to catch it. Reena would often say, "If you don't catch the ball and it hits me, you'll have to do fifteen minutes of extra stretching." I never knew if she was serious or not. Obviously, I made sure never to drop the ball.

Alex's style of therapy was different. He used brute force and pushed my ankle forcefully. Although I needed both styles of therapies, it was no secret that I enjoyed Reena's therapy and dreaded Alex's. At the end of a session with Alex, I was often in tears. In the car, I would wonder, "Is this all worth it?"

I was becoming angrier and angrier. The pain was making me irrational. At times, I would start talking to the frames, telling them how much I hated them. By the third week of December, I was losing my sanity. I kept telling Dad, "When the frames come off, I want to burn them." One day I was complaining about the frames and telling Mom and Dad how many things the frames on my legs prevented me from doing. I said, "I can't sleep on my sides. I have to keep away from the kids- my nieces Ria, Reshma, Roshni, and my cousin Juhee- for the fear that they might bump into my frames."

Dad told me I should not concentrate on what the frames were preventing me from doing. Instead, I should think about what they were helping me achieve. He said, "These frames are making you taller, a half a millimeter every day." I knew he was right. But when you are in pain, logic goes out the window.

Overall, things were as well as they could be. My cousin Paroo came to see me from London on December 18. My other cousin Anisha was coming from London for Christmas holidays to cheer me up.

I wasn't throwing up anymore and my range of motion was very good. Mom and Dad were suggesting that we should try to get ten more days and get five more millimeters out of this surgery. I knew they were right but I also knew that I could not take a minute more after January 5˙

We had one final appointment to see Dr. Rozbruch on December 22. We were in a festive mood, not only because it was Christmas, but because so many things had gone right for me. We wanted to express our appreciation to many people. For Christmas, we gave a TiVo to Alex. For Reena, we got a Sony camcorder. For everyone else at JCPT, we got a bottle of champagne.

On the morning of December 22, first we went to JCPT for an hour and a half of therapy with Alex. There we gave our gifts to Alex and Reena, and a bottle of champagne to every worker at JCPT. There was immense joy in our hearts. We were thankful to everyone and thankful to God. We needed to share our joy.

We then headed off to New York. Once in New York, we first got the x-rays done. This time, we had even more things to carry with us. We had brought our laptop with us, along with the DVD movie of my therapy. We were also carrying a full carton of champagne bottles, enough for everyone in Dr. Rozbruch's office and two for Dr. Wagner's office. Of course, for Dr. Rozbruch himself, we got Dom Perignon.

While we were in Dr. Rozbruch's waiting room, we ran into a young Indian doctor, Dr. Lalit Shah. We had never seen him there before. Mom and Dad were writing labels on each of the bottles. The Indian doctor introduced himself. He was going to do limb lengthening in India and he wanted to learn from the best.

As we had done every other time, we would hand the x-rays to the receptionist, who would then give it to Dr. Blyakher. He took the x-rays in his office and started measuring the amount of distraction. In the mean time, we were handing out champagne bottles to the staff. Everyone in Dr. Rozbruch's office was genuinely touched. Just then, Dr. Blyakher stepped into the reception area and said, "The x-ray measures forty-two millimeters of extraction."

"What?" said Dad with disbelief.

"Oh no, no," he corrected himself. "It measures fifty-eight millimeters, but you have to take 10 percent out because of the enlargement during the x-ray. That will bring it to about fifty-two millimeters," said Dr. Blyakher.

Dad took a sigh of relief and said, "Fifty-two millimeters is exactly where my chart says he should be."

In the examination room, the Indian doctor came in with a young Chinese doctor. Then Dr. Fragomen and Dr. Blyakher came in. There was a festive atmosphere in the room. Everyone was happy about my remarkable recovery from the setbacks of November. Dad set up the laptop and started showing them the therapy movie. It was a graphic and brutal depiction of the therapy. Even though they were doctors, they were gasping. Now they knew how I salvaged this very tough situation into a moderate success.

Just then, Rozbruch walked in. Dad quickly started the movie from the beginning. Rozbruch's eyes were glued to the computer screen. When the movie ended, he said, "These people really know what they're doing. Many therapists are afraid to use the force that is necessary. These guys," he said laughingly, "have just the right amount of sadistic energy." He had seen pictures of my therapy with Alex, but this was the first time he had seen Reena. He turned to me and with a grin on his face, said, "Akash, good job getting a pretty therapist."

Everyone in the room agreed with Rozbruch's assessment and laughed approvingly. I said, "That makes it easier to take the pain. But don't be fooled by her looks. She's a tough cookie." Then I told him about one of my early visits with Reena.

Reena would make me walk some fifty steps as one of the routines. On that particular day, with a walker in my hand and Reena by my side, I was slowly inching forward. Reena, in a rapid-fire motion, was yelling her instructions. "Back straight, heels down, relax your shoulders, butt in, don't lean to your side." Another patient of Reena's, standing on the side, turned to my dad and said jokingly, "With all this much nagging, I think your son is ready for marriage now."

Rozbruch laughed. That was it! We had achieved our mission. Not only had we made him laugh, we made him realize how extraordinary the quality of my therapy was. Rozbruch said, "I would like to put a movie like this on our website." He then started examining me. I told him about a pin that was bothering me. He said it looked fine. He checked my ankle movement and seemed satisfied. He then looked at me and said, "The question you will ask is, do we stop here or do you keep going?"

"Damn, you're good! You must have gone to medical school or something," I said.

He said, "Akash, you have worked so hard, and we think you should go up to sixty millimeters and get one full centimeter more than what you were going to get."

That was good news, but he had previously okayed up to fifty-eight millimeters anyway. Therefore, he was giving us only two more millimeters. We were greedy and wanted as much more as safely possible. Dad asked, "What if we slow things down?" This was of course a trick question. The purpose was to find out whether Rozbruch was agreeable to a surgery date after January 5.

Rozbruch said "No, we can't slow things down because after January 5th, I don't have any openings until mid- February."

"What if we speed things up?" asked Dad.

"No. We can't do that either."

"His ankle motion looks so good," said Dad. "Can't we shoot for three inches?"

"Three inches is possible for somebody who starts at five feet two or five feet three. It is a matter of percent increase. The same percent would give higher increase to someone who started a few inches taller than Akash," said Dr. Rozbruch.

"In that case, once we reach our goal, what if we take a few days off and see how he's doing?" Dad wasn't giving up.

"I am so fully booked. If we miss January 5th, I won't be able to see him until March," he said in a tone that indicated an end of discussion.

That was that.

As we left his office, we were happy that my lengthening would continue for two more millimeters but disappointed that Rozbruch's mind was made up about stopping there.

Dad then rushed to see Ross Saddler, the head of the Accounts Receivable department at the hospital. It was a short yet productive meeting. Dad told him that the hospital should settle at $100,000 for three surgeries. Ross said he would give us his final answer in a few days.

All throughout the ride home, I was very tense. I wanted the surgery to take place on January 5. Dad wanted me to get a few more millimeters and wanted to see if the surgery could be postponed until January 10. The very thought of delaying the surgery even by a day made me sick to my stomach. I was arguing with Dad about why it was better to do it on January 5. "You just don't understand what I am going through," I said in a stern voice.

Dad did not say anything. Mom, Dad, and I were all very agitated. Then, once on the turnpike, Dad said, in a beat-up, crushed voice, "I'm fighting so hard to change Rozbruch's mind about this. I can't fight on two fronts at the same time. If I have to convince both of you, then this can't be done." His sincere words touched me. But I was too tired from the pain and torture of the last three months. I did not say anything.

Once home, when I was alone in my room, I looked at my frame. They were clinging to my legs with the help of screws and wires. I started talking to them. I was losing my mind. I said, "I want you to leave me- leave me alone. But Dad is right. I will never have this opportunity again where I can grow taller at will- half a millimeter a day. I will put up with you, you bitches, for a little while longer."

I wiped my tears and called Dad. I said, "Dad, give me a hug." Then as he hugged me, I said, "As much pain as I'm in, and as fed-up as I am of this surgery, I understand what you are saying. This phase will never come back again in my life. I can grow, at will, a half a millimeter a day, every day. Once the rings are off, this magical period will come to an end. Go ahead, try to convince Rozbruch. I don't mind a few more days here and there. Just don't make it a few more months."

Dad said, "Are you sure?"

"Yes, I am sure," I said. "That does not mean I won't bitch and moan a lot. But I am sure."

The next morning, Mom, Dad, and I kept discussing what would be the right thing to do. We reviewed our past conversations and what we had read. There was a sense of emergency in our household. There were some errors you make where it would be easy to recover. In this case, there was no way to recover. We could not insist on doing anything against Dr. Rozbruch's advice. On the other hand, if we did not fight hard enough, there was no way I could ever again, in my entire life, recreate this situation where I could grow half a millimeter every day. The stakes were high, either way.

We remembered that when I first saw Dr. Rozbruch, he had told us we should select the external fixator over ISKD mainly because ISKD would be set to two inches ahead of time and no matter how well things were progressing, you could not get anything more. With the fixator, on the other hand, he said we would have the freedom of making corrections to our schedule as we went along. We had debated for weeks as to whether or not I could put up with the fixator. The ISKD would have been clean. Once the surgery was done, there would have been nothing sticking out of my body. There would not have been a daily torture of pin care. There would have been no fear of infection. At night, I would not have to put seven pillows around my legs to keep them straight. But the ISKD would not have allowed the freedom of making corrections along the way. That was one of the two reasons why I had opted to take the additional pain and suffering. Now was the time to take advantage of that sacrifice.

Dad said, "All we are asking for is ten or fifteen more days. We had a setback in late November. Everything is fine now. This time will never come back again in your life." He said, "Rozbruch has to do whatever it takes to make sure we're not rushing into the second surgery." Dad spent the whole next day composing a letter to Dr. Rozbruch.

Dr. Rozbruch had said, if a patient starts at five feet three inches can gain a maximum three inches, or an increase of 4.76 percent. I started at four feet eleven and a half inches. The same percent increase should give me 2.8 inches. With the quality of therapy I was receiving, my range of motion was getting better by the day and I thought I could go for a little more.

Before Dad sent the letter, he gave it to me and asked me, "Do you agree with everything? Only then will I send it."

I read it and said, "Yes." It wasn't an enthusiastic yes. It was a yes from my mind, even though my heart wanted to get it over with very quickly. Here is the letter:

Subject: Surgery Date

Hello Dr. Rozbruch,

It was a good visit Tuesday afternoon, and we want to express our thanks one more time for treating Akash and us with such grace, humor, and professionalism.

On the way back home, Akash talked at length about his final height. He was somewhat down that he would miss the mark of five feet two inches by a few millimeters. The scheduled surgery date will take him to sixty millimeters. I am writing this letter to see if there is anything you can do to change the date of surgery by seven days.

In many ways, Akash is tremendously conflicted about this. On one hand, he wants the pain and torture of the pin care and the therapy to be over. He wants the fixators out as soon as possible. On the other hand, he knows that he is in a miraculous phase of his life where his height is increasing by half a millimeter every day.

Then there is the emotional investment by the entire family. Apart from the out-of-pocket cost of around $170,000, Akash has endured an unbelievable amount of pain. Meena works with Akash from early morning till late at night. I took a three-month leave-of-absence from my job as CEO of S.S. White Technologies. With that kind of commitment of time and resources, I hope you can see why we would like to push this project to its absolute safe limits. If we can get even a half a millimeter more by rescheduling, we would not mind the additional wait. Of course, it would be a question of whether your schedule would have that kind of flexibility. I am hoping that you could make a special arrangement for an early morning or late evening, but continue the lengthening until we reach the safe limits. I know Akash told you he would be happy with reaching two inches. That was before he started the gruesome, torturous therapy at JCPT twice a day. Akash's range of motion is getting a little better with every passing day. The therapists at Jersey Central think that they can maintain Akash's range during the distraction phase.

This morning, I read an article in the November issue of *Journal of Bone and Joint Surgery* titled, "Complications Encountered During Lengthening." It suggests that the probability of complications goes up with a lengthening of over sixty millimeters, but the article only included the IM (ISKD) method and not the Ilizarov method. The mean length increase for forty-two cases in the study was sixty-three millimeters. That actually gives me a reason for hope. With the first-rate care Akash is getting from you and your office, the overdose of the top quality therapy he is getting from the guys at JCPT, and the careful attention he gets from Meena and me, it would seem reasonable to expect that Akash should be able to exceed the mean increase reported in the study. If his ankle/knee motion continues to remain satisfactory and the bone growth appears to be normal, what other risks would we encounter by pushing this for another week or so?

Dr. Rozbruch, I am sorry that I keep pushing this. We want to make sure we do not leave a single millimeter on the table before moving to the next phase. Can you do something to give us that peace of mind? Any special consideration from you will never be forgotten. In our own small way, Akash, Meena and I will do everything we can to be enthusiastic spokespersons for this procedure. We will forever remain goodwill ambassadors for the limb lengthening procedure. We will be in your debt and will make sure we make it up to you.

If you think we need to discuss this more, please let me know. I know you are going to be away for the Christmas break, so if there is any possibility of rescheduling, it has to be done now.

Hope to hear from you soon,

-Rahul Shukla

The e-mail was sent on Thursday, December 23, at 12:38 p.m. Dr. Rozbruch sent a reply immediately, but to Dad's office e-mail address. Thankfully, Dad could not check his e-mail for the next three days. Here is his response:

Dear Shukla family,

The article you read was not about stature lengthening for CSS. Sixty millimeters of lengthening in a patient who is starting at four feet eleven inches is a huge lengthening because

it is about percent increase. Lengthening for
equalization or in dwarfism is much easier. We
are truly pushing the envelope and he will
likely need heel cord releases. It's not a good
idea to go any further. I have already gone further, and this will be the largest percent
lengthening for CSS that we have done.

The next surgery is four hours (half day)
that has been set aside. Omaira tells me that
we are scheduled into March at this point. She
is away this week. Jessica is in. (Jessica can
look at the schedule to see if there are any
unexpected openings.) I don't see how I can delay the surgery for seven days unless I do this
from eight p.m. to two a.m. This is obviously
not optimal and further lengthening is also not
optimal. Also, further delay in leaving the
fixator on is not optimal. So, for many reasons, we should stick to our plan.

I know that you have a lot invested in this,
as do I. You will have achieved an amazing
thing and most importantly, we do not want to
compromise function.

Happy Holidays. Don't slack off on the PT.

S. Robert Rozbruch, MD

We pretty much knew at that time that this phase of the surgery
was now over. In a way, we were all very happy that it was. I think we
were all completely spent. Dad wasn't ready to give up quite yet. He
said, "I have to try one more time. I have to convince myself that
we've pushed this matter to its limits. I would never forgive myself
otherwise." So he sat down and wrote one more letter. He said, "This
is the very last try. If he says no, we will accept it and start celebrating
the great success we have achieved so far." The letter went out on
Tuesday, December 28, at four thirty p.m.

Subject: A last long letter from Shuklas

Hello Dr. Rozbruch,

Thanks for your detailed response. I did not check my mail at my work-address until yesterday. We read your response only yesterday.

I understand and appreciate your caution. As for my persistence, that is how God has manufactured me. I had to work on my wife for four years before she agreed to marry me. In 1988, when the company I worked for was being sold, I called bank after bank, begging for a loan for six million dollars, and ended up buying the company. My wife thinks my persistence is tiring. But I am working on her to make her change her mind about that!

If, in your professional opinion, we should not go any farther with Akash's distraction, then that is fine. We are mentally prepared now for the distraction to end on the 4th and the surgery to take place on the 5th of January. If, on the other hand, a slot opens up between now and the 4th- for the surgery on the 10th or the 12th -and if you want to re-evaluate if Akash can safely undergo three or four more millimeters of distraction, then I am sure you will instruct us to reschedule.

The reasons for my persistence on this matter are many folds: On the mathematics of percentage increase, Akash is fifty-nine and a half inches tall. I understand that the average height for patients for this kind of surgery is sixty-four inches. That is only a 7.6 percent difference. Thus if a person sixty-four inches tall can achieve fifty millimeters under normal circumstances, and seventy-five under the most ideal circumstances, then Akash, with his height, should be able to achieve from the normal forty-six millimeters to an ideal sixty-nine millimeters.

My second reason for optimism is how well his therapy is proceeding. Both therapists (Reena and Alex) at JCPT have indicated that Akash's range is very good. Even during the holidays, JCPT opens specially for Akash and puts him through three hours of vigorous therapy every day. I cannot imagine any other patient having the access to as much and as good a therapy as Akash does. It may be useful for you to call Alex and get a first-hand update. If nothing else, you can instruct them on the post-surgery therapy for after the 5th of January.

When we discussed this matter with Dr. Paley two years ago- and with you six months ago- we had heard that a very well-motivated patient can go up to three inches. Since we knew how well-motivated the Shukla family was, we were hoping for the best. But I fully agree with your statement, "Most importantly, we do not want to compromise functions." Since Akash's range seems okay now, I surmise that your concern is based on what you might have seen in prior cases. Maybe you have seen cases where pushing it beyond sixty millimeters created complications. If you share that information with us, we would be able to intellectualize this better.

That is all, Dr. Rozbruch. We will go to HSS on the third for the pre-op and see you on the 5th. If you see any change in your schedule or want to see Akash before the 5th, please let us know.

We agree that together we have achieved an amazing thing. Please do not think that we are not excited about this. Hope you and your family are having happy holidays.

-Rahul Shukla

While waiting for a reply from Dr. Rozbruch, we were also waiting for a response from Ross Saddler regarding the hospital bills. His response came on the 28th. He agreed to a round number of $100,000 for all three surgeries. We had paid $65,000 so far. Mom put $35,000 on her American Express on the 29th. It was a happy conclusion to a major challenge. December 29 was also the day we received Dr. Rozbruch's response.

Dear Shukla family,

I'll plan to see you on the 5th. Keep working hard on the ankle/knee stretch and we'll decide about the soft-tissue release. I have seen patients from elsewhere end up with significant ankle complications. We have had an organized, rational, enthusiastic, and intelligent plan. Let's get these frames off and the bones healed. I will contact you if anything changes.

S. Robert Rozbruch, MD

Even though he said no, we were happy and relieved. We had a great joy of knowing that we had exhausted every option. It would be a shame if Dr. Rozbruch was wavering about which way to go and we did not persuade him to go our way. At least now, we knew that there was no doubt in his mind. Our e-mail campaign wasn't a failure after all. By writing two strong letters, we now had inner peace. We knew that there was nothing else we could have tried. That created tranquil-ity in us. Dad had a smile on his face. Mom looked happy. And I started counting the days when the fucking frames would be removed.

The rings- the black and ugly rings- had made my life a living hell. But they did make me two and a half inches taller. Now that the rings were coming off on January 5, a burden was lifted off our souls. It was a tense two days when we were trying to convince Dr. Rozbruch to give us a few more days. When he said no, in a way it created a con-clusive end- a successful one- to my tough journey. We were in a celebratory mood.

On New Year's Eve, at eleven thirty p.m., we sat down in my room to watch the New Year's ball descend at Times Square. Mom kept a bottle of champagne and three champagne glasses ready. Yes, I know I was not twenty-one yet. But with what I had gone through that year, they wanted me to have a few sips. At 12:01, Dad popped the cork and poured the champagne in three glasses. We rang the glasses. With tears welling in his eyes, Dad said, "It was a tough year, but we did well. The tough year is behind us."

Indeed!

With tears of joy, we hugged one another and said, "Happy New Year!"

28 F*cking Rings Come Off – The Second Surgery

On the morning of January 5, I got up at six thirty and got ready quickly. I had taken a shower the night before and was not supposed to eat anything before the surgery. Just before we left, we lit the candle-like lamp in front of the statue of the gods and said our prayers. We left at seven forty-five. The traffic was bad on Route 78. The anxiety of the surgery was making us a little short tempered.

As we were getting on the Turnpike from Route 78, Dad's cell phone rang. It was Sushi Auntie. She said that my cousin from England, Reena, called right after we left home. Reena is my mom's younger sister's daughter. She was twenty-six and an osteopath. She loves to sing and dance and has a wonderful rhythm about herself. Only last year, Reena and I performed a song together at my other cousin's wedding. She has a sunny personality and a loving heart. In 1995, Reena and her sister Anisha spent two weeks with us, and we all went to Disney World together. Since then, I have been very close to both of them.

Mom, Dad, and I were wondering why Reena had called. I picked up my phone and called her. She said, "I called to wish you good luck." She asked me if I was nervous.

I said, "Do cows give milk?"

She laughed. She said, "Don't be." And then she told me she had just lit a candle and said a prayer for me. Such affectionate thoughts were making me less nervous about what I was going to face in an hour.

By nine thirty, we were sitting in front of the admissions clerk on the fourth floor. The hospital bill for this surgery and the one that was to follow were already paid for in full on December 29. Therefore, the admissions process moved along much faster. The woman on the other side of the counter was asking me a lot of questions. I told her the purpose for the surgery. "I grew two and a half inches," I told her.

"Oh my God! They can do that?" she said. I glanced at Dad. We had the same reaction from the admission clerk the first time around. We were thinking this must not be a very common surgery at all. The admissions clerk at the best orthopedic hospital in the country had not heard of this surgery. That made me feel very special but somewhat scared.

We went to the atrium and waited for my name to be called. It was a short wait. A nurse walked in and said, "Is Akash Shukla here?"

My heart skipped a beat. I knew that soon they would start sticking needles and stuff in me. The next few days would not be fun. Mom and Dad pushed my wheelchair to my pre-operative room. It was the same room I was in on September 24. There was a beautiful view of the East River. It seemed like I was watching a rerun of a TV show. Dr. Rozbruch stopped by at 10:25. He must have finished the first surgery of the day. He was wearing blue scrubs and a sterile hat.

I said, "I'm loving that hat, by the way."

The people in the room laughed. He then asked me, "Are you ready to rock and roll?"

"I've never been more ready," I replied. He checked my ankle motion and told us, "Let us do the tissue release." Dad and Mom nodded. A tissue release would mean that they would make an incision on the back of the leg, above the ankle on the muscle called the gastrocnemius muscle. It is a powerful muscle that is in the back part of the lower leg and runs from just above the knee to the heel. Cutting this muscle would restore my ankle flexion and bring the motion closer to neutral.

Months ago, Dr. Rozbruch had explained that there was always a small danger in damaging the nerve. "Having said that," he said, "I have done this many times and never had a patient experience nerve damage." He had also said when we prepaid for the surgery, "If I end up doing the tissue release, I'm not going to nickel and dime you to death. I will not charge you for that part of the surgery." I wasn't sure if I wanted the additional pain of a tissue release, but if Dr. Rozbruch said I needed it, I was sure I did. Rozbruch then wrote his initials on both my legs.

At about eleven, Dr. Wagner walked in. He had the same reassuring smile as the last time we saw him. He said, "I'll be administering the anesthesia." Just knowing that he would be in the operating room was very comforting for me.

Soon two nurses came to take me away. Mom and Dad gave me a hug and told me not to worry. "Look who's talking." I said, knowing that I'd be fast asleep and they'd be doing all the worrying. We proceeded to Operating Room 4. The OR was just as damn cold as the last time.

I wish I could describe what the OR looked like, but because of my nervousness, I have no memory of what it looked like inside. I remember my latest x-rays were hanging on the wall. One of the doctors said, "The bone formation looks great." As they were preparing me, someone said, "I remember working on you last time." Another voice then said, "Me too." This was good. I was in familiar hands.

Dr. Wagner stood near my head and said, "Okay, Akash, we are going to get started."

I said, "Just let me know what I have to do."

He replied jokingly, "I want you to lose consciousness once I inject this serum in you." We both laughed. In his hands, he held a syringe with a six-inch-long needle. The size of the needle terrified me until I realized that he wasn't going to poke me with it- he was going to inject it into my IV tube. They quickly transferred me from the stretcher to the operating table. The serum that Dr. Wagner had injected was causing a severe burning sensation. I was wondering when Dr. Rozbruch would walk in.

The next thing I knew, I woke up in the recovery room. I knew the surgery was done. My back felt very cold. I had an epidural catheter in my back. I also knew that I had a urinary catheter, but I couldn't feel it. I couldn't wait to see my legs without the black ugly frames. I lifted my head up but a nurse from far yelled at me to keep my head down. She couldn't have the slightest idea how badly I wanted to see those black metallic frames gone. They had become so much a part of my anatomy that in a weird way, it was difficult to imagine my legs without them.

My mouth was so dry that I thought the roof of my mouth would crack. As the nurse walked by me, I mustered up enough energy to call her. She gave me some ice chips. I asked her when I would be able to see my parents. She said, "Visiting hours for the recovery room start at six p.m. It's five thirty."

Prior to all of this and while I was still in surgery, my mom and dad, along with Uncle Rajen, Aunt Neha, Aunt Rekha, Sushi Auntie, and Cousin Asit, were anxiously waiting in the atrium. This huge hall with an enormous glass window overlooking the East River was on the same floor as the recovery room. All throughout the day, there were about forty or fifty people sitting in the waiting room. Every half an hour or so, you would see a doctor come in from the surgery room, find the appropriate relatives, and give them an update on how the surgery went. My family waited patiently as one after another family got the news. Lots of families hugged each other with relief when they got the good news about their loved one.

I was taken in the OR at eleven a.m. My family had not gotten any word from anybody until three fifteen p.m. Mom and Dad were getting nervous. Why was it taking such a long time? Then Dr. Blyakher walked into the atrium and walked towards Dad with a black metal frame in his hands. Prior to the surgery, we had asked if I could keep at least one of the frames as a souvenir. So here was Dr. Blyakher, handing my dad the crazy souvenir I had requested. Dad jumped up from his chair, asking, "Has everything gone all right?"

Dr. Blyakher replied, "Everything's fine. You will soon hear from Dr. Rozbruch."

Dad held the ring in his hand and kept staring at it. "How much pain this ring has inflicted on my son," he was thinking.

Uncle Rajen asked Dad, "Why are you so sad?"

Dad said, "I'm not sad. Looking at this ring makes me realize what we have been through." He then handed his video camera to Uncle Rajen and said, "Take a movie of me looking at this frame. This is a benchmark moment."

The receptionist behind the counter started walking towards them. She then said in a stern voice, "Sir, please don't take any movies."

Dad turned to her and explained gently, "We are taking the movie such that nobody else in the room is in the frame, just me and my family." As Dad was talking, she started walking away. Dad thought that she accepted his explanation.

Within minutes, Dr. Rozbruch walked in, smiling from ear to ear. He said, "Everything has gone exactly as it should have. No complications. The IM rods are in and he's doing well."

Mom and Dad collectively breathed huge sighs of relief. Dad again gave the camera to Uncle Rajen and asked Dr. Rozbruch, "Please repeat what you just said- this time for the benefit of the camera."

Dr. Rozbruch knew the passion of the Shukla family for capturing every moment of this surgery on video and he happily obliged. Once the camera started rolling, with a chuckle and playfulness, he repeated what he had just said. But the receptionist looked very unhappy. As Dr. Rozbruch started walking out, she jumped to her feet and stopped Dr. Rozbruch outside the atrium on the other side of the glass wall. Dad couldn't hear what she was saying, but from her expression, he figured out that she was complaining about us taking a movie. How ridiculous this woman was! This receptionist- Dad to this day refers to her as the "bitch receptionist"- had no business complaining to Dr. Rozbruch. Here we had a doctor who was humoring us, going along with our silliness, and this bitch had to make him feel uncomfortable. But the matter did not end there.

A few minutes later, the head of security came to the atrium, walking toward the receptionist. She pointed towards my dad. The security officer approached Dad and said, "Sir, please don't take a movie in the atrium."

Dad is not the kind of guy who easily gets intimidated. He said to the security officer, "Why don't we talk about it in the hallway?" Once in the hallway, Dad calmly, but in an authoritative voice, explained the kind of surgery that I had gone through. He said, "My son is writing a book about this experience. Even your own hospital gave us special permission to have one of the product managers from my company stay in the OR to take pictures. I don't understand how the movie I take here of my family and my doctor is of any concern to the hospital."

The security officer said, "It's a privacy issue."

Dad said, "But if I'm taking a movie of only my own family, how am I violating anybody else's privacy?"

"I guess you're right," he said. "It's just that there are hospital rules, only to protect you."

Dad said, "Officer, my family is paying for the surgery, not the insurance company. I'm one of the few people who have paid in full for all three surgeries in advance. Do you know how much this surgery is costing us?"

The officer was getting curious by this time. "How much?" he asked.

"Two-hundred thousand dollars," Dad told the officer. The officer gasped. Dad said, "You don't mind if we take a movie of what is happening with us, do you?"

"Go ahead, sir." He shook Dad's hand and left.

At six, Mom came into the recovery room. She gave me a hug and said, "Dr. Rozbruch said everything went very well." She held my hand and asked, "Are you in a lot of pain, Beta?" I nodded a painful yes. With a helpless look on her face, she said, "I'll tell the nurse to get you some more pain killers."

Next Dad came in. He leaned, gave me a gentle hug, and said, "I am so very proud of you- you did it!"

I said, "Dad, I want the pain to end."

He held my hand with one hand, touched my hair with the other hand, and said, "The hard part is over!"

29   The Hard Part Is Over

Compared to the first surgery, the days in the hospital after the second surgery were rather uneventful. Dr. Rozbruch came to see me the next day, January 6. He was all smiles. He said, "Things went well, beyond the best expectations." He moved my ankle to neutral position and said, "See? Because of the release, you're already back to neutral."

The biggest disappointment for me was that the pain had not gone away. I had been waiting for the rings to come off so badly that in my mind, I had created this expectation that once the rings were gone, the pain would 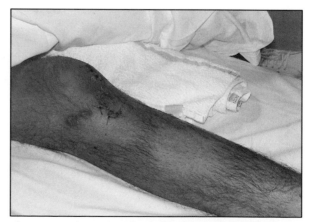 be gone. Such was not the case. As a matter of fact, on January 6 and 7, there were several times when the pain seemed more severe than right after the previous surgery.

The two catheters were making me very uncomfortable. When the nurse came to give me a blood thinner shot in my stomach, I asked her, "When can I get the catheters out?"

She said, "You'll have to discuss that with the anesthesiologists."

When the anesthesiologist came, he said it was pretty much my decision. Once he left, Mom, Dad, and I talked about it and decided I was better off without these things sticking in my back. We told the nurse at four p.m. that I was ready to have both catheters removed. She came in at five thirty to remove them. She told me slowly to roll on my side. Once I did, she removed the first catheter. I didn't feel a thing. She told me to get on my back. "Now I'm going to take your urinary catheter out." Needless to say, the removal of the urinary catheter hurt a lot!

Once the urinary catheter was removed, I needed to pass urine within eight hours (by two a.m. that night) or else they would have to reinsert it. By nine p.m., I had not passed any urine. Dad looked ready to pass out. Mom kept his spirits up by saying, "Don't worry. It'll happen soon." Thankfully, at eleven, I filled half a bottle. Needless to say, I was relieved- in more than one way.

I ate my first solid food- crackers and potato chips- on Thursday, January 6 at nine p.m. and my first bowel movement was at twelve thirty that night (in order to give the reader an exact idea of the timing of key events, look how I have to humiliate myself!).

The pain somehow seemed much worse; I don't know why. The first session with the physical therapist was the evening of January 6. I couldn't stop shivering afterwards. My teeth were chattering very loudly. It seemed like I was going to go into shock. Dad held my hand. With tears in my eyes, I said, "So much pain, Dad, so much pain."

Dad said, "Let's talk about something pleasant." He then started talking about our frequent trips to Disneyland from when I was young.

The IV needle was still stuck to my arm. They don't like to take it out unless your health has completely settled. On Friday, January 7, at one p.m., the IV needle came out. Now there was nothing sticking into my body.

By that time, Mom was doing more physical therapy with me than the physical therapists. During the first surgery, we were not very knowledgeable about the kind of physical therapy I'd need. By now, Mom could probably teach a course on it. Mom and Dad helped me move to the edge of the bed so that I could dangle my feet. This time, the hospital had put a shoe-like device on my feet. With air pressure, it would squeeze different parts of my foot at regular intervals. This would help the circulation and prevent blood clotting. I had to keep it on all the time. There were times where it hurt so much that I had to remove it for a short while.

On Saturday, January 8, the therapy went better than expected. The therapist, Carlene, asked me to stand with my shoes on. Once I did, she said, "99 percent you'll go home tomorrow."

The kids in our family came to see me. At first, the security guard would not let them up. Visitors under the age of twelve were not allowed. As the security guards were stopping my nieces, a nurse was passing by. The kids are absolute charmers. She started talking to them and then told the security guard, "I'm taking them upstairs." The therapist wheeled me to the waiting area where the kids were 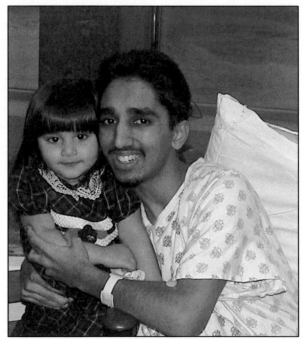 waiting for me. They gave me hugs and kisses. Dad took many pictures of me and the kids. I could see in the pictures how thin and bony I looked. In the last one month, I had lost twenty pounds. Before the first surgery, I weighed a hundred and five pounds. On January 8, that day in HSS, I weighed eighty-five pounds.

On Sunday, January 9, Dr. Drakos, one of Dr. Rozbruch's residents, came to examine me. He said, "I'm going to let you go today." He proceeded to sign all of the release papers and left them at the nurses' station. At eleven a.m., the head nurse came and wanted me to sign some of the discharge papers. By this time, Mom had already helped me get dressed. I slowly transferred into the wheelchair. It felt strange not to have the black rings affixed to my legs. At noon, Dad pulled the car in front of the patient pick-up. Mom wheeled me downstairs. She placed the wheelchair parallel to the front door. With great difficulty, I lifted one leg and put it in the car. I then moved my body onto the car seat. Then I did the same with my other leg. The contrast with how things were the first time around was profound.

Then it was a familiar route: FDR Parkway, to the Holland Tunnel, to the Turnpike, to Route 78, to my hometown, Warren. We had started talking about this surgery some three years ago. For a long time, it was a great dilemma whether I should go through this or not. Then on September 24, I went to New York for my first surgery. They took a healthy, able-bodied person and cut the leg bones in half. They put mean, ugly rings on my legs. They drilled holes and put screws into my flesh and bone. The screws oozed blood. Pin care would bring me closer to insanity every day. The rings stayed on for three months.

The car was speeding away on the New Jersey Turnpike. I could not stop staring at my legs.

The black ugly rings were gone. I could not believe it was over.

30 Tough Withdrawal from Painkillers

reached home at four p.m. The journey from the car to my room was much less painful and took a lot less time than the first time. That night, when I went to sleep, Mom did not have to put mounds of pillows on either side of my legs. I was able to sleep on my side. For a while, it had seemed that this day would never come.

The next weekend, the New York Giants were playing in the playoffs. I could watch the game in my "hospital room," in our family room, or downstairs on the one-hundred-thirty-five-inch screen in the home theater. I asked Mom if I should try crawling down the steps. She said, "Sure, go ahead and give it a try."

I transferred from my bed to the wheelchair and rolled the chair to the edge of the staircase. With some help, I stood up, took one step forward and sat down on the top step. I lifted my upper body off the ground with both my hands and shifted my behind down one step. Dad stood in front of me, ready to catch me if I started falling. I crawled downstairs like a one-year-old. It wasn't difficult at all. The whole thing lifted my spirits. I had become mobile. I was not confined to just one floor.

That night, I discussed with my parents if I could start sleeping in my own room on the second floor. The last time I had slept in that room was on September 22. For the last three and a half months, I had slept downstairs in a hospital-like room. Not just me but both my parents had moved into the same room during this entire period. From that night on, we all started sleeping in our own rooms.

On January 15, Mom took me to JCPT for therapy. What a warm welcome I received. It was the hard work of the people at JCPT that gave new life to my impossible project. Reena, Alex, Caroline, Jennifer, and Jaime all had taken my situation personally. First, the project was stopping at thirty-six millimeters, then at fifty millimeters, then at fifty-five millimeters, and finally we took it to sixty millimeters. This was an incredible journey. It was a fantastic success story. So on the day of my return to JCPT, they all were smiling from ear to ear. They felt that it was as much their own success story as it was mine.

Ever since I was back from the hospital, we were working on reducing my intake of painkillers. While in the hospital, I took 4 mg of Hydromorphine every three hours. Once home, I continued the same schedule till January 8. From January 9, I took 2 mg, three times a day. By January 12, I had stopped taking Hydromorphine cold turkey and relied strictly on Tylenol. By January 15, the pain was getting bad. I started taking 2 mg of Hydromorphine twice a day.

All was not well. I looked better but did not feel better. I complained a lot about pain in my back, thighs, and hips. Oddly, the pain from the surgery wounds seemed to be under control. The pain in my hips, at times, was unbearable. On January 16, at the breakfast table, I found my left leg shaking at my knee. Dad told me to stop shaking my leg. I shouted, "I'm not doing it. It's happening by itself." I was uncharacteristically disagreeable. Then I yelled, "You just don't understand. This is not an easy surgery." Then suddenly I broke into sobs. We were confused as to what was happening to me.

For the previous three days, I had extreme difficulty sleeping and got up at five in the morning. I would be restless for the rest of the day. During the worst pain of this surgery during the previous four months, I could always count on *Friends* and *LA Law* to divert my attention. Not this time. Nothing was working. Dad started wondering if I was suffering from withdrawal from all the pain medications.

In an e-mail to Dr. Wagner, Dad wrote, "Akash seems very withdrawn and very quiet. When the pain gets bad, he moves his upper body in a rhythmic motion and makes strange faces. Sometimes he keeps shaking his legs and says that makes him feel better." Dad asked Dr. Wagner if I was suffering from withdrawal symptoms. Mom and Dad were extremely worried about what I was going through and requested an urgent response from Dr. Wagner. The e-mail was sent at 12:02 p.m. on Monday, January 17.

Dr. Wagner responded within eight minutes. He said that indeed, I was going through withdrawal from too rapid a tapering off from the pain medication. He suggested that I take four pills a day for a week, then reduce it to three per day for a week, then two per day for another week, and then once a week for the last week. He said, 'You can use Tylenol and get off Hydromorphine entirely but in that case, you will have withdrawal symptoms for three to four days.'

I discussed with Dad if we could come up with a compromise schedule. The pace Dr. Wagner had suggested would take a month to taper off. I wanted to do it quicker. My cousin Meetali, who had married in June, was coming to visit us with her husband, Poshin, on January 28. I wanted to make sure I was my old self by then. We came up with a schedule where I would take four pills for one day, three pills for the next two days, two pills for the next three days, and one pill a day for the last four days.

Dr. Wagner was right. It was indeed withdrawal symptoms. Once I started following the new schedule for easy tapering off, everything turned out okay.

The recovery was mostly uneventful, except for January 26. In the evening, as soon as Dad came home from work, he said, "Let's watch TV in your recovery room." By "recovery room," he referred to the room where I had spent three and a half months. We could have just as readily sat in the family room to watch TV. Why did Dad suggest my old room? I did not give it much thought. Why was he saying, "Let's watch TV before dinner"? I did not give that much thought, either.

Johnny Carson had died only a few days ago. We had recorded on TiVo Jay Leno's tribute to Johnny Carson. We went to my room and started watching it. Fifteen minutes later, the bell rang. Dad quickly got up and went to answer the door. He came back with a smirk on his face and said, "Akash, somebody is here to see you." I thought it must have been one of my high school friends. I transferred from my bed to the wheelchair and got out of my room and into the hallway. Dad had stepped out first. I saw him standing at the far end of the kitchen with his camcorder rolling. In a second, someone entered the kitchen and started walking towards me. I could not believe my eyes. It was Reena, my dear cousin from England. I kept saying, "Oh . . . my . . . God . . . ."

Reena and I were very close. Throughout the surgery, she called me frequently to lift my spirits and to give words of encouragement. She was my pillar of strength during this surgery. When her younger sister, Anisha, was here, Reena had said she wanted to come see me very badly.

Here she was, standing in front of me. I could not believe this was for real. I gathered all my strength, stood up to give her a hug, and almost broke into tears. Mom and Dad knew about Reena's plans. They had arranged for a limo to pick her up from the airport. Every detail about how Reena would walk in the house, where Dad would stand, and how they'd bring me in from the room into the kitchen was all pre-planned. If we had been watching TV from the family room, I would have seen Reena enter the house. That was the reason why Dad suggested we watch TV in my old room. I had a splendid time with Reena. Two days later, my other cousin,

Meetali, and her husband, Poshin, came. For the next two days all of us had a blast.

For the next one month, I went for therapy once a day. I also continued my vigorous routine at home. On February 15, we went for a follow-up visit to see Dr. Rozbruch. We were back on the familiar roads. It felt strange being on that road and not being in as much pain. At the previous appointment, Dr. Rozbruch had told us, "Next time you are here, I will tell you if you can fully bear weight." If he gave me permission to bear weight, I would not have to use the wheelchair and I would start walking with a cane. I was hoping he would say yes to that.

As usual, we first went to the radiology building and got my x-rays. As it had become our routine, on our way out from the radiologist's office and in their hallway, Dad would take the x-rays out, hold them against the window, and study how the point of incision looked. That day we all agreed that the bone formation, where we had created a gap in the bone, looked pretty good. We could clearly see the rods that were inserted through my knee and the bone screws that were holding them in place.

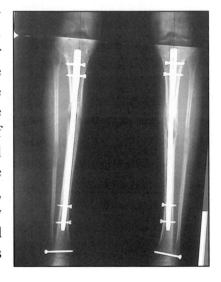

Once we got into Dr. Rozbruch's office, we went into one of the examination rooms. Dr. Rozbruch came in a few minutes later. He said, "X-ray looks very good." Then he said, "Let's see if you can walk."

I got up slowly. I was a bit nervous. I had not walked unassisted for the last four months. I had difficulty maintaining my balance. He said, "It's okay- you can hold my hand because we're friends." I grabbed onto his hands and walked slowly. I walked down the hallway and back to the examining table. He paused for a moment and then said, "Okay. I am going to give you permission to walk."

That evening when I went to JCPT, we did not take our wheelchair with us for the first time. At the parking lot, I got out of the car. I had a cane in my hand. I walked slowly but confidently. It felt as if I was flying. Dad held the entrance door to JCPT. I walked towards the reception desk. Alex's wife, Caroline, was sitting at the receptionist's desk. When she saw me walking towards her, she jumped up from her seat. She yelled, "Reena, Reena, take a look. Take a look."

Reena, from the other end of the hallway, had a huge grin on her face and yelled back, "I'm looking, I'm looking." Their faces were beaming with joy.

My melancholy days were coming to an end.

31   Was It All Worth it?

I started driving again in mid-March. For the first few days, I would have Mom or Dad sit in the passenger seat. They would check my reflexes by asking me to stop suddenly. They wanted to make sure I had enough strength to apply the brake. On March 31, I drove by my-self to JCPT.

Later that evening, I thought about going to Bridgewater Commons Mall. I asked Mom if it would be a good idea to go to the mall by myself. I wanted to feel my newfound freedom. She thought about it for a few seconds, then a smile flashed on her face. "Sure!" she said.

Once at the mall, I parked the car on the rooftop parking lot and walked to the mall entrance. The place was as packed as I remembered. I had missed the hustle and bustle like this for the last seven months. On my way to the food court, I had to first pass the AMC Theater complex. I felt different with my new height. I was five feet two inches now. I had purchased shoes with a two-inch heel, making me five feet four. That was not a towering height, I know, but it was a height that allowed me to more readily blend.

I stopped to look at the movie posters on the wall. As I started walking away, towards the food court, I saw this beautiful girl waiting in line to buy her ticket. She had tied her dark brown hair with a white scrunchie. She wore a tight blue long-sleeved Hollister t-shirt, which accentuated her very nice figure. Suddenly she turned her face to me and saw me looking at her. As our eyes met, I flashed a smile.

She did not turn her face away.

She smiled back, a friendly, warm, and inviting smile. As I passed her, I smiled back- a brief, gentle, confident smile. Suddenly I felt an unusual serenity inside me. It was just a casual smile from a stranger. But it meant much more to me. Her smile represented an acceptance- a kind of a promise that now I was free to engage the world as myself. I was simply Akash, instead of "short."

I walked away from her and toward the food court, thinking that this surgery had been one of the most painful experiences in my life. They broke my bones with a chisel, drilled holes in my flesh and bone, and inserted screws and bolts. We turned the struts on the frame every day and stretched my body ruthlessly. The pins would ooze blood. Daily pin care was brutal. The physical therapy was painful to the point that I thought I would pass out.

Writing this book was not easy. It brought back vivid memories of that horrible time of my life.

And now that you, the reader, have read all about the gruesome account of what I went through, you may want to ask me the question, "Was it all worth it?"

As I was walking away from the AMC Theater in Bridgewater Commons, happy about the warm friendly smile from the pretty girl wearing a blue Hollister t-shirt, I knew the answer to the question was a resounding yes.

The End

Me and my Mom before the surgery

Me and my Mom after the surgery

Height Change Over 12 weeks

Six weeks later

12 weeks later

Day before the surgery

10 weeks later

Watch the words come alive at
www.MeasureofAMan.us

Many of the intense moments described in this book were also captured on video and by photographs. The sights and sounds are organized on the website by chapter numbers in this book. Please visit **www.MeasureOfAMan.us**

Appendix

Table 1: The original distraction schedule

	Day	Red 1	Orange 2	Yellow 3	Green 4	Blue 5	Violet 6
10/4/2004	0[#]	192	204	197	204	185	200
10/5/2004	1	193	205	198	205	186	201
10/6/2004	2	194	206	199	206	187	202
10/7/2004	3	195	207	200	207	188	203
10/8/2004	4	196	208	201	208	189	204
10/9/2004	5	197	209	202	209	190	205
10/10/2004	6	198	210	203	209	191	206
10/11/2004	7	199	211	204	210	192	206
10/12/2004	8	200	212	205	211	193	207
10/13/2004	9	200	212	206	212	194	208
10/14/2004	10	201	213	207	213	195	209
10/15/2004	11	202	214	208	214	196	210
10/16/2004	12	203	215	209	215	197	211
10/17/2004	13	204	216	209	216	198	212
10/18/2004	14	205	217	210	217	199	213
10/19/2004	15	206	218	211	218	200	214
10/20/2004	16	207	219	212	218	201	215
10/21/2004	17	208	220	213	219	202	216
10/22/2004	18	209	221	214	220	203	217
10/23/2004	19	210	222	215	221	204	217
10/23/2004	20	211	223	216	222	205	218
10/25/2004	21	212	224	217	223	206	219
10/26/2004	22	213	225	218	224	207	220
10/27/2004	23	214	226	219	225	208	221
10/28/2004	24	215	227	220	226	209	222
10/29/2004	25	215	227	221	227	209	223

		Red	Orange	Yellow	Green	Blue	Violet
10/30/2004	26	216	228	222	227	210	224
10/31/2004	27	217	229	223	228	211	225
11/1/2004	28	218	230	224	229	212	226
11/2/2004	29	219	231	225	230	213	227
11/3/2004	30	220	232	226	231	214	228
11/4/2004	31	221	233	227	232	215	229
11/5/2004	32	222	234	228	233	216	229
11/6/2004	33	223	235	229	234	217	230
11/7/2004	34	224	236	230	235	218	231
11/8/2004	35	225	237	231	236	219	232
11/9/2004	36	226	238	232	236	220	233
11/10/2004	37	227	239	233	237	221	234
11/11/2004	38	228	240	233	238	222	235
11/12/2004	39	229	241	234	239	223	236
11/13/2004	40	230	242	235	240	224	237
11/14/2004	41	231	243	236	241	225	238
11/15/2004	42	231	243	237	242	226	239
11/16/2004	43	232	244	238	243	227	240
11/17/2004	44	233	245	239	244	228	240
11/18/2004	45	234	246	240	245	229	241
11/19/2004	46	235	247	241	245	230	242
11/20/2004	47	236	248	242	246	231	243
11/21/2004	48	237	249	243	247	232	244
11/22/2004	49	238	250	244	248	233	245
11/23/2004	50	239	251	245	249	234	246
Intercept		192.0	204.08	197.12	204.09	185.23	200.07
Slope		0.936	0.9364	0.9553	0.8982	0.9706	0.9171
Degree to Fit		99.9%	99.96%	99.96%	99.95%	99.97%	99.96%

Table 2: Extended strut positions based on table 2 values

Intercept		192.08	204.08	197.12	204.09	185.23	200.07
Slope		0.9364	0.9364	0.9553	0.8982	0.9706	0.9171
Degree to Fit		99.96%	99.96%	99.96	99.95%	99.97%	99.96%
Day	51	240	252	246	250	235	247
	52	241	253	247	251	236	248
	53	242	254	248	252	237	249
	54	243	255	249	253	238	250
	55	244	256	250	253	239	251
	56	245	257	251	254	240	251
	57	245	257	252	255	241	252
	58	246	258	253	256	242	253
	59	247	259	253	257	242	254
	60	248	260	254	258	243	255
	61	249	261	255	259	244	256
	62	250	262	256	260	245	257
	63	251	263	257	261	246	258
	64	252	264	258	262	247	259
	65	253	265	259	262	248	260
	66	254	266	260	263	249	261
	67	255	267	261	264	250	262
	68	256	268	262	265	251	262
	69	257	269	263	266	252	263
	70	258	270	264	267	253	264
	71	259	271	265	268	254	265
	72	260	272	266	269	255	266
	73	260	272	267	270	256	267
	74	261	273	268	271	257	268
	75	262	274	269	271	258	269
	76	263	275	270	272	259	270

Epilogue

In April of 2005, there was a small ambulatory surgery to remove one bone screw from each leg. By that time, my walking was completely back to normal. I took a summer job at Home Depot as a sales representative. Although the pain was gone, my family and I were still recovering from the shock of what I had gone through. That fall, I started my first year at Drexel studying Mechanical Engineering. The extra two and a half inches of height made a dramatic difference not only in the way I looked, but also in my confidence.

Occasionally, I would have nightmares that the frames were back on my legs and I was back in the lengthening phase. I would wake up in a cold sweat, feel my legs and would be relieved that it was only a dream. But within three months, all my bad memories of the surgery had gone. Such was not the case with my Mom and Dad. In December 2005, Dad was driving to a friend's house when he passed Williams Surgical. He broke into instantaneous sobs. Mom and Dad went through a very difficult recovery for the next two to three months.

The IM rods and the remaining screws were removed in March of 2006 in another ambulatory surgery. After that, we talked less and less about the surgery. That summer, Dad's company had enrolled eighty-three employees to run in a statewide 3.1-mile run. I planned to only walk the course; however, once the race started, I forgot all about my surgery and ran like I used to in High School. Out of eighty-three people, I finished ninth. My family and I officially got over the trauma

of the surgery. Any doubts whether this surgery would have any long-term effect on me were completely gone.

In 2007, the New York Post was doing an article on limb lengthening and wanted a quote from me. When they talked to me, they found my story so fascinating that they did the entire article about my surgery. A Canadian filmmaker, Howard Goldberg, contacted me about being in a documentary called *Short & Male*. The crew spent a day at my house and the documentary came out in May of 2008. That same year, during the company 5K, I finished fourth out of the eighty-five employees. By this time, the scars on my legs were completely gone. The latest bone x-ray would give no indication of where the lengthening occurred. When relatives and friends ask me if I have mild pain or discomfort, I tell them that my legs and the bones are as normal as they were before the surgery.

During my co-op cycle of spring/summer 2007, I interned for my Dad's manufacturing company and enjoyed the Industrial Engineering work a lot. I decided to switch majors and transferred from Drexel University to NJIT in Newark, NJ.

When I started at Drexel, the memory of the surgery was still lingering. At NJIT, that memory has completely faded. I am a confident man. I don't think about my height a lot. That is the true dividend of this surgery. I participate in many extra-curricular activities at NJIT. I write for the school newspaper, I started my own singing group, and I give tours of the campus to potential students. I have made many good friends at NJIT and—although I have not found the right girl yet—I am not shy to approach girls the way I used to be.

Things turned out quite all right. I am a lucky man.

Getting This Book Published...

I've already expressed my gratitude throughout this book to the professionals who helped me get taller. Here I want to thank people who helped me with writing the book.

Thanks to Carolyn Ketcham, Madhu Rye and Mary Beth Parlato for correcting my manuscript and giving me many suggestions. Thanks to the people at Llumina Press, particularly Debbie Dawson for her guidance and Fina Florez for the beautiful layout of this book.

This book would not have happened at all without the help, guidance (and nagging) from my Dad. He encouraged me to write, guided me on every aspect of the book and tirelessly edited my writing. His wisdom and emotions made my words much more powerful. Thanks Dad.

-Akash Shukla
September 30, 2008